Red-headed Woodpecker

Birds
of the
St. Louis Area

*where and when
to find them*

by the
Webster Groves Nature Study Society

Birds of the St. Louis Area
Where and When to Find Them

Published by the Webster Groves Nature Study Society
P. O. Box 190065
Webster Groves, Missouri 63119-6065

ISBN 0-9643406-0-7

Designed and printed by Murray Print Shop, Inc.

Front cover: Eurasian Tree Sparrow *(Passer montanus)* in Choke Cherry *(Prunus virginiana)*; painting by Chuck Witcher.

Contents

Maps

Colored Illustrations

This is the fourth publication about the birds of the St. Louis area. The first was *Migratory and Permanent Resident Birds in the St. Louis Region*, by Sterling P. Jones, published by the St. Louis Bird Club in 1943. The 16-page book (revised in 1947 to 20 pages) listed arrival and departure dates, with some species listed as rare or casual. The second effort was a 40-page book, *Birds of the St. Louis Area*, by Eugene J. Wilhelm, Jr., published by the St. Louis Audubon Society in 1958. The book used a code system to indicate relative abundance and seasonal status of each species. It also indicated earliest, latest, and peak dates for all migrant species and commentary on many species. In 1968, Richard A. Anderson and Paul E. Bauer completed *A Guide to Finding Birds in the St. Louis Area*, a 44-page book published by the Webster Groves Nature Study Society. The book used a bar-graph format to indicate the relative abundance and seasonal distribution of each species. It contained comments on the status of most species, but dates of specific records were included only for species of accidental occurrence. Major birding areas were described, with details about directions, what birds to expect, and the best time of year to observe them. A map of the St. Louis area and six regional maps were included to show details of birding spots mentioned in the text. A common feature of each of the three previous books was a history of the Eurasian (formerly European) Tree Sparrow in St. Louis.

This new *Birds of the St. Louis Area* has the same title as the 1958 book and follows the same general format as the 1968 publication. Descriptions of old birding areas have been updated, new areas have been added, and information on the abundance and seasonal status of each species has been updated. The maps have been redrawn to show new highways and new birding areas. There is now an account for each species that has occurred in the area, including those that are extinct, extirpated, introduced, or of insufficiently documented occurrence ("hypothetical"). The species accounts discuss the normal habitats, records of unusual occurrence, and the best locations for finding each species. In an effort to appeal to newcomers, visitors, and casual bird lovers as well as experienced local birders, we have added some new features. These include sections on attracting birds to the yard, organized birding activities, and a "glossary of named places, local jargon, and abbreviations."

Obviously, there have been many changes, both in birding areas and bird status, during the 27 years since Anderson and Bauer (1968). Twenty-two bird species have been seen in that time that are new to the area, including the House Finch, which has become one of the most common birds at feeders in the last ten years. The number of gulls and the diversity of gull species has increased, while some other species have decreased in abundance. A new birding area, the Riverlands Environmental Demonstration Area, has become the new "hot spot" while an old hot spot, the levee region in Monroe County, Illinois, has cooled. Birding areas and bird status will continue to change. At this writing the flood of the summer of 1993 has had a profound influence on large portions of the area. Some regions have been altered permanently and there will be changes in land use that will undoubtedly affect the birds as these regions recover. These changes will provide a focus for bird students preparing the next edition of this book.

Preparation of this book was initiated in 1990 when several members of the Webster Groves Nature Study Society (WGNSS) began discussing the revision of *A Guide to Finding Birds in the St. Louis Area*, by Dick Anderson and Paul Bauer, a 1968 book that was both out of date and out of print. In July of 1991 a self-appointed team, "The Bird Book Committee," first met to lay plans to prepare a revision. The five committee members listed below are those who met regularly for the next four years to research, assemble, structure, write, and edit this book. However, many WGNSS members and other people have contributed their time and expertise to its completion. With their help, this book has become considerably more than just a revision of the earlier book.

Much of the information on bird occurrence presented here is based on records of many area birders published over the years in *Nature Notes*, the journal of the Webster Groves Nature Study Society. In particular, the many years of valuable monthly articles by Rose Ann Bodman and the late Earl Comfort in *Nature Notes* summarizing interesting bird sightings was the source of most of the new information since the previous book.

Bill Rowe provided information and text for the **SPECIES ACCOUNTS, BIRDING LOCATIONS**, and **SEASONAL OCCURRENCE** bar graphs, as well as acted as proofreader and editor for several early drafts of these chapters. Ron Goetz contributed much information for the **SPECIES ACCOUNTS** and **SEASONAL OCCURRENCE** chapters as well as assisted in editing early drafts of some of the text. Proofing of most of the final version of the text was generously provided by Kevin Renick. The Committee members, however, take full responsibility for any errors or inconsistencies.

Additional crucial data on bird records were contributed by Dave Becher, Jean Cook, Mark Peters, Phoebe Snetsinger, and Jim Ziebol. Text and information for some of the birding locations were provided by Dick Coles, Bill Rowe, Judy Tisdale, and Helen Wuestenfeld. Many of the maps were augmented with computer generated overlays produced by Cindy Lippincott, to whom we owe a special thanks. Some of the typing chores were shared by Theresa Goetz and Ruth Kopp.

The artwork for the front cover was supplied by Chuck Witcher. Jim Ziebol and Carmen Patterson donated the sketches which supplement the text. We are particularly indebted to these talented artists.

The Committee and the Webster Groves Nature Study Society extend their appreciation and thanks to the above contributors.

In addition, we thank Peggy Leonard and Robert Gaddy for their valuable production, financial, and legal advice. We are particularly appreciative of Nancy Webb and Tim Alton of Murray Print Shop for rescuing the production of this book and Lisa Wester for her design expertise and patience through the production stages. Finally, we thank Ed Barresi for his vision, enthusiasm, and generous contributions.

The Bird Book Committee:

Connie Alwood
Dick Anderson
Paul Bauer
Randy Korotev
Jack Van Benthuysen

St. Louis, Missouri
April 17, 1995

The Webster Groves Nature Study Society

The city of Webster Groves, Missouri, is one of the oldest "suburbs" of St. Louis. Shortly after World War I, citizens of Webster Groves and members of various garden clubs were invited to a meeting by Alfred F. Satterthwait to form an organization to study nature. The result was the formation of the Webster Groves Nature Study Society in 1920 with 115 members. The society has grown to become the principal organization of amateur naturalists in the St. Louis area. For historical reasons the name has remained unchanged, although at this writing there are about 500 members scattered throughout the St. Louis area and several states.

The main interests of the original assemblage were entomology, botany, and ornithology, and these three interest groups still form the core of the organization. Each group has regular field trips and meetings, and the Society at large meets monthly to enjoy lectures by guests or members knowledgeable in diverse aspects of nature study.

In 1930 the Society began a journal, *Nature Notes*. Over the years, hundreds of members have contributed their observations, knowledge, and personal experiences to the publication. Announcements and reports of meetings and field trips are regular features.

The stated objectives of the Society are "to stimulate interest in nature study on the part of adults and children, to cooperate with other organizations in nature study, and to encourage amateur research in the natural science." In keeping with these objectives, field trips and meetings involve the exchange of knowledge between experienced and inexperienced members. Interaction between amateurs and professionals is encouraged. The Society also helps support the Field Science Program at the Tyson Research Center, a program that introduces St. Louis school children to their natural heritage. It contributes research scholarships to college students and helps send teachers to Audubon field camps. Contributions to other nature organizations are also made. Other activities include the coordination of two Christmas Bird Counts for the National Audubon Society and the maintenance of the recorded telephone message "Nature Line" to inform the community of recent interesting bird sightings.

All those with an interest in nature are invited to join. Please direct membership inquiries to The Webster Groves Nature Study Society, P. O. Box 190065, St. Louis, Missouri 63119-6065.

King Rail with young

irds have held a natural appeal through the ages that transcends barriers of age, culture, geography, and politics. With the increased awareness of the impact of humanity on the ecology of the planet, interest in birds has also increased in recent years. For example, the Missouri Department of Conservation estimates that more than 70% of Missourians watch birds at their homes.

The St. Louis area is rich in bird life and an exciting place to enjoy birds. There is no better place in the country when it comes to ease of finding or seeing large numbers of certain bird species. Barred Owls and Pileated Woodpeckers, common year-round residents of the riverbottom forests, are joined by large numbers of Yellow-throated and Prothonotary Warblers in summer. Bald Eagles occur by the hundreds along the Mississippi and Illinois Rivers in winter. Worm-eating and Kentucky Warblers, difficult to find in many other parts of the country, fill the Ozark forests with song in May and June. And (of course!) there are the Cardinals and Eurasian Tree Sparrows. More than 370 species of birds have been seen in and around St. Louis and new ones are found every year as the natural wandering of birds brings new species to the area and more people are looking for them.

This book is intended to be helpful to anyone with an interest in the birds of St. Louis and the surrounding area. It is primarily directed at birders — people who enjoy observing birds, learning about birds, and actively seeking the diversity of birdlife the area has to offer. (As has become customary, we call such people "birders," a term most serious birders prefer to "birdwatcher" because "watching" is only one way to enjoy birds.) The book should be useful to birders at any level. It will help backyard birders determine which bird species are most likely to be seen at their feeders and when to look for them. Beginning birders will learn about the seasonal changes in St. Louis bird life, as well as the habitat different species prefer. Birders new to the area will discover the local hot spots, while out-of-town birders will learn where to seek birds on their "want lists." Experienced resident birders will find information on the best times to look for the rarer species. Even the arm-chair birder may find some unexpected surprises about species that occurred in the St. Louis area a hundred years ago.

Because there are already numerous good resources available to aid in bird identification, this book is not a "picture book" and is not intended as an identification aid. It should be used in conjunction with a good field guide. Those field guides most useful in the St. Louis area are described under "Identification Aids" in the final chapter.

GEOGRAPHIC SCOPE

The geographic region covered by this book is limited to the "St. Louis area," which is defined as the area *within 50 miles of the nearest border of the city of St. Louis.* This definition is arbitrary, but one of long standing tradition among St. Louis birders. By this definition, the St. Louis area is nearly circular in shape, measures approximately 117 miles from north to south and 107 miles from east to west. At approximately 9800 square miles, the St. Louis area is bigger than the states of Maryland, Massachusetts, or New Jersey. Out-of-towners and newcomers should note that as a political unit, the city of St. Louis does not lie in St. Louis County and is only a small portion of the greater metropolitan area.

GEOGRAPHY

Three major rivers, the Mississippi, the Missouri, and the Illinois, join north of St. Louis. These rivers are major features of the geography of the region and are major factors influencing its bird life. The Mississippi and Illinois Rivers, along with their bordering riverbottom forests and bluffs, serve as corridors for birds migrating north and south, while the Missouri River channels some western birds to the area, such as American White Pelican and Prairie Falcon. The Illinois River also serves as a link to the Great Lakes and provides a route to St. Louis for many gulls. Floodplains of the great rivers provide low-lying agricultural land and riparian habitat that host many bird species. Some of the most accessible floodplain lies in eastern St. Charles Co., Missouri, the narrow strip between the Mississippi and Missouri rivers north of the city. Two major oxbow lakes, Horseshoe Lake in the Mississippi River floodplain of Illinois and Marais Temps Clair in St. Charles Co., accommodate the best remaining marshlands in the area. Along the Illinois River, Swan Lake, another large oxbow, is part of the area's only National Wildlife Refuge.

The St. Louis area contains the last three dams on the Mississippi River, No. 25 at Winfield, Missouri, No. 26R at Alton, Illinois, and No. 27 at Chain of Rocks, just south of the I-270 bridge in north St. Louis. Below Dam No. 27, where the elevation of the river is normally about 400 feet above sea level, the river is free flowing to the Gulf of Mexico. These dams act to concentrate numerous species of birds, particularly in winter. The Mississippi River makes a large bend to the east around St. Louis. From most residential areas of St. Louis city and county, a crow flying south, east, north, or even northwest will reach the Mississippi River. This geographic quirk is probably responsible for many bird sightings in the densely populated central portion of the area.

Above the Mississippi River floodplain to the east lie the relatively flat and productive farmlands of Illinois. This area was once prairie, and some prairie bird species are still common (Horned Larks, Dickcissels). Besides occasional coal mines, the major disruptions on this landscape are the Kaskaskia River and two artificial lakes that lie along the river, Carlyle and Baldwin. The Kaskaskia River acts as a north-south corridor for migrants through central Illinois, and the lakes act as traps for numerous water birds. Carlyle Lake, the biggest lake within Illinois, also appears to act as a trap for migrating landbirds, which are often found in higher-than-average numbers along the lakeshore during migration.

As one crosses the Mississippi River from Illinois to Missouri, the landscape changes abruptly. West of the Mississippi River and north of the Missouri River is a region dominated by rolling hills with mixed forest and farmland. Southwest of St. Louis is the rugged

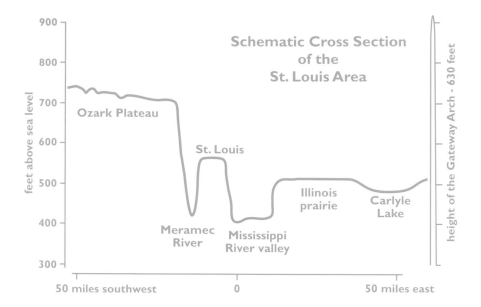

Schematic Cross Section of the St. Louis Area

900
800
700 — Ozark Plateau
600 — St. Louis
500 — Illinois prairie / Carlyle Lake
400 — Meramec River / Mississippi River valley
300

feet above sea level

height of the Gateway Arch - 630 feet

50 miles southwest   0   50 miles east

Ozark plateau. The Missouri and Mississippi Rivers are at the northern and eastern extremes of this ancient mountain range. Within 50 miles of St. Louis, the highest elevations reached are 1100 feet. The Ozarks are cut by numerous streams; in the St. Louis area the largest Ozark stream is the Meramec River. Vertical distances between the Meramec River and adjacent hilltops are as great as 400 feet. Some characteristic species of the Ozarks are the Yellow-throated Warbler (along the streams), Worm-eating Warbler (valleys), and Prairie Warbler (uplands).

St. Louis lies at the edge of the normal range of several species, and these boundaries are in part related to local geography. As discussed in more detail in the **SPECIES ACCOUNTS**, the boundary between the ranges of the Black-capped and Carolina Chickadees passes through the area and, in Missouri, the boundary seems to be influenced by the Missouri River. St. Louis is near the northern boundary of the summer ranges of such species as Fish Crow and Bewick's Wren and of the winter range of Field and Savannah Sparrows. Similarly, it is near the southern boundary of the summer range of Sedge Wren, Henslow's Sparrow, and Yellow-headed Blackbird. The Black-throated Blue Warbler is at the western extreme of its migration route. The birds of St. Louis are primarily birds of the eastern United States, but a few western species occur regularly (White Pelican, Prairie Falcon).

THE EURASIAN TREE SPARROW

The Eurasian Tree Sparrow is a unique resident of the St. Louis area. The primary range of this Eurasian species in the United States is restricted to St. Louis city and several surrounding counties. Birders throughout the country make a special point of visiting St. Louis to see it and add it to their "life lists." As a special resident here for over 120 years, the Eurasian Tree Sparrow deserves a brief historical review.

South St. Louis was the home of many German immigrants who wanted to see familiar birds from their homeland. Twenty Eurasian Tree Sparrows were released on April 25 of 1870 in Lafayette Park in south St. Louis (Widmann, 1909). Numbers of European Goldfinches, Bullfinches, Chaffinches, Greenfinches, and Linnets were also released, but only the Eurasian Tree Sparrow successfully established a breeding population. In 1878 came the invasion of the more aggressive House Sparrow (another European immigrant), which began to push the Eurasian Tree Sparrow from its established nesting areas. Both species are actually in the family known as weavers and are unrelated to our native sparrows. Expansion of the city also caused the Eurasian Tree Sparrow to spread, for it prefers suburban areas and open country. Today, there are still individuals in the city and a fair number in the suburbs, but most of the range expansion has been to the north, along the Illinois and Mississippi River valleys.

The species now commonly breeds in St. Louis and St. Charles Counties in Missouri, and Madison and Calhoun Counties in Illinois. It is reported that it is as common as the House Sparrow in Meredosia, Illinois, 75 miles north of St. Louis. Small numbers have also been found farther north. Burlington, Iowa, reported fifty birds at a feeder in the winter of 1991-92, and in Pierce County, Wisconsin, a single bird returned to a feeder each winter for five years through 1992. Since the exact range and population of the species is not known, there is considerable work to be done by bird students. For example, what is the effect on the population of Eurasian Tree Sparrows from the recent invasion by House Finches?

The Eurasian Tree Sparrow builds a somewhat thatchy nest, sometimes in the eaves of houses. It often visits feeders and sometimes a few are seen mixed in flocks of House Sparrows. However, in winter it often groups with others of its kind, and flocks of over 100 birds can be seen in rural areas, often near water or in hedgerows or brush.

The Eurasian Tree Sparrow is easy to identify, but one useful point is omitted by most bird guides — the narrow white nape collar (see cover), partial or complete, which serves as a quick distinction from the House Sparrow at some angles. See the **SPECIES ACCOUNTS** for the best areas in which to find the Eurasian Tree Sparrow.

OTHER INTRODUCED SPECIES

Most Americans can trace their ancestry to Europe, Africa, or the Far East. Some of our birds are not indigenous to this country, either, and St. Louis has several bird species in addition to the Eurasian Tree Sparrow that were introduced, most in the 19th century. One of these, the Cattle Egret, arrived on its own without the help of humans in the 1960's; the others were deliberately brought here and released. Some of these, most notably the Rock Dove, European Starling, and House Sparrow, are now considered nuisances because they are numerous, compete for nest holes with native birds, or are "untidy" in large numbers. Because it consumes crops, the Monk Parakeet is such a nuisance that it is destroyed in some areas of the country. It first appeared in our area in the 1970's and has not yet become established, although a few individuals are occasionally seen. More information on introduced species is given in the **SPECIES ACCOUNTS**. The following is a list of the introduced species that occur in the St. Louis area.

Species	Origin
Cattle Egret	*Africa, via South America*
Mute Swan	*Europe*
Ring-necked Pheasant	*Asia*
Rock Dove ("pigeon")	*Europe*
Ringed Turtle-Dove	*Europe*
Monk Parakeet	*South America*
European Starling	*Europe*
House Sparrow ("English sparrow")	*Europe*
Eurasian Tree Sparrow	*Europe*

Although not "introduced" in the same sense, the House Finch is also an immigrant to St. Louis. It is a species native to the arid southwest United States that was released on the east coast in the 1940's. From the east it spread westward and became common in the St. Louis area during the 1980's.

ORGANIZATION OF THIS BOOK

This book should be used, not just read. We hope
that it will spend a lot of time in the car or by
the kitchen window next to the field guide,
not on the bookshelf. Thus, it has been
designed to travel as well as to be a
convenient source of information.
The information is presented in six chapters. Following this **INTRODUCTION**
there is a short chapter on
**ORGANIZED BIRDING IN ST.
LOUIS.** Most of the remainder
of the book consists of three
large parts. **BIRDING LOCA-
TIONS** describes the best places to
see birds in the St. Louis area. The
chapter is supplemented by a set of maps
to help direct birders to the locations.
Next comes the **SPECIES ACCOUNTS**,
which lists each of the 370 species that
have been seen in the area and provides

House Finch

some information about their status. Then, in a chapter designated
SEASONAL OCCURRENCE, information on the relative abundance of each
species through the seasons is presented in graphical form. Finally, in a
short chapter entitled **ENJOYING BIRDS AT HOME**, we provide some information useful to people who feed birds or want to attract birds to their
yard.

Scarlet Tanager

any people enjoy birding by themselves or with a friend as a means of getting away from the crowd, but for those who occasionally enjoy birding in groups or for new birders who wish to learn from more experienced birders, there are various opportunities in the St. Louis area. In addition to organized field trips, there are two annual birding events, Christmas Bird Counts and "Big Day," that have become a tradition among area birders.

FIELD TRIPS

The Webster Groves Nature Study Society has regular birding trips on Thursdays and Saturdays; these are announced in the monthly newsletter, *Nature Notes*. During the course of a year most of the areas discussed in this book are visited. Newcomers and nonmembers are always welcome. The St. Louis Audubon Society also sponsors periodic birding field trips that are announced in their newsletter (or call 314-822-6595).

CHRISTMAS BIRD COUNTS

Christmas Bird Counts are sponsored by the National Audubon Society as a means of censusing the winter population of birds in North America. The first count was held in 1900. Presently, there are over 1600 counts with over 43,000 participants held throughout the United States, Canada, Mexico, and the tropics. The rules are simple. A single day is chosen within a period of about two weeks in late December and early January. As a group, participants count all the birds they can find in a circle 15 miles in diameter during the course of the day, keeping strict tabulation of numbers of individuals of each species and numbers of hours and miles spent walking and driving. Individual participants are usually assigned to parties of a few people that cover a portion of the count circle. Many count circles have been long established, and counts that have been held in the same area for many years are particularly valuable as a means of monitoring long-term changes in bird distribution and abundance. Christmas Bird Counts offer some sport because it is a challenge for one party to find a rarer species or a greater number of species than another and, as a group, to find a high total number of species for the count circle.

Several Christmas Bird Counts are held in the St. Louis area. The Pere Marquette count (Illinois) covers Pere Marquette State Park and portions of the Mark Twain National Wildlife Refuge that lie in Calhoun County. The Orchard Farm count (Missouri) covers much of the floodplain of eastern St. Charles County and a portion of northern St. Louis County. These two counts have been held nearly every year since the 1930's. The Orchard Farm count typically records high numbers of Eurasian Tree Sparrows (342 in 1992). The Weldon Spring count (Missouri) includes the Busch and Weldon Spring Conservation Areas of western St. Charles County and portions of nearby St. Louis County. This count was initiated in 1951. Prior to 1986, only the Busch Area was censused, but since then the whole circle has been covered. The Elsah (Illinois) Christmas Bird Count covers the campus of Principia College and the Mississippi River along the Great River Road in Jersey County. Most of Horseshoe Lake is included in the Collinsville (Illinois) count circle in Madison Co.

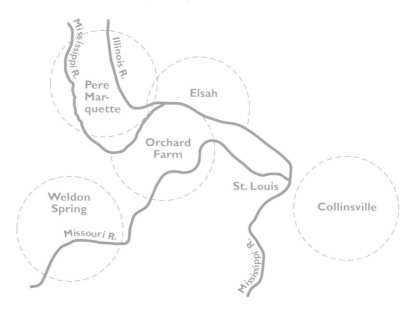

Dates for Christmas Bird Counts are announced in *Nature Notes*, the journal of the Webster Groves Nature Study Society. The more people that participate, the more successful a count will be. New participants are always welcome. The National Audubon Society requires a participation fee ($5, at this writing) in order to help defray the expense of preparing the large report in which the results are published each year.

SPRING COUNTS

The North American Migration Count (NAMC) is a fast-growing birding activity that began in 1992. The purpose is to monitor the distribution, abundance, and status of migrant birds. All counts around the country are held on a single day, the second Saturday in May, in order to obtain a "snapshot" of the progress of the spring migration. It is similar to a Christmas Bird Count in that participants count numbers of each species, but instead of covering a 15-mile-diameter circle the area of each count is an entire county. The NAMC is not sponsored or affiliated with any established organization, but is coordinated by volunteers who compile the results and publish an annual newsletter summarizing the results. However, the Illinois Department of Conservation has been conducting an essentially similar count in Illinois for many years with volunteer support. Information on the NAMC can be obtained from the originator and coordinator, Jim Stasz, P. O. Box 71, North Beach, MD, 20714. The event is announced in *Nature Notes*, with information on local participation.

BREEDING CENSUSES

Some birders participate in other organized bird censuses. Surveys of breeding birds are done each summer at the Tyson Research Center. The U. S. Fish and Wildlife Service solicits volunteers for their Breeding Bird Survey, which involves counting birds in June along a preassigned automobile route, some of which occur in the St. Louis area. Both Missouri and Illinois have had Breeding Bird Atlas Projects in which volunteers sought evidence of breeding (nests, fledged young) in blocks of land selected randomly around each state. Although both Atlas Projects are completed, they may be revived at a later time to determine if there are any changes in breeding status.

BIG DAY

While birders participate in Christmas Bird Counts and spring counts as an entertaining way to collect useful data, they do "big days" purely for the sport. The goal of a big day is for an individual or group of birders to identify (see or hear) as many different species in 24 hours as possible. In order to compete with each other, St. Louis birders traditionally do  a big day on a Saturday in early May, the time of year that the greatest number of species occurs in the area. By tradition, birders must stay within the 50-mile limit defined here as "the St. Louis area." Routes are carefully planned to maximize the numbers of species seen, and many groups start very early in the morning and continue until after dark. In a good year, a group may find more than 160 species and the record by all participants on a single day is 193. Some birders also do less competitive big days in September when as many as 120 species have been found. In the same competitive spirit, many area birders keep lists of the number of species they have seen in the area for each calendar year. High totals typically run over 230, with a record of 276.

OTHER AREA BIRD ORGANIZATIONS

Persons seeking information by mail about wild birds in the St. Louis area can contact the Webster Groves Nature Study Society at P.O. Box 190065, St. Louis, Missouri 63119-6065. Information may also be obtained from the St. Louis Audubon Society. At this writing, St. Louis Audubon does not have a permanent mailing address, but the most recent address can be found in the Greater St. Louis telephone directory. The principal statewide birding organization of Illinois is the Illinois Ornithological Society, which publishes *Meadowlark - A Journal of Illinois Birds*. Send inquiries to Illinois Ornithological Society, P.O. Box 1971, Evanston, IL 60204. In Missouri, statewide records of bird sightings are maintained by the Audubon Society of Missouri and published in their quarterly journal, *The Bluebird*. Inquiries about the Audubon of Missouri can be sent to the Webster Groves Nature Study Society.

RARE BIRD INFORMATION

For information on recent bird sightings in the St. Louis area, call the Nature Line for a recorded message. The Nature Line is sponsored by the Webster Groves Nature Study Society. For information on rare bird sightings in other areas of Missouri and Illinois, call the respective rare bird alert.

Nature Line	*(314) 935-8432*
Missouri Rare Bird Alert	*(314) 445-9115*
Central Illinois Rare Bird Alert	*(217) 785-1083*

Carolina Wren

Cerulean Warbler

ne of the fascinating aspects about enjoying birds is that birds can be found almost anywhere. People who work at Barnes Hospital see Peregrine Falcons on window sills, motorists on I-270 see Canada Geese or even Wild Turkeys flying across the freeway, and on slow nights at Busch Stadium, baseball fans who tire of the Cardinals can watch American Kestrels and Common Nighthawks catching insects attracted to the lights. It's easy to observe a variety of interesting birds without going to much effort, just by watching and listening during the normal course of a day.

Nevertheless, for those interested in the maximum diversity St. Louis has to offer, some locations are particularly good places to see birds. The locations described on the following pages are the most popular birding spots among St. Louis area birders. This does not imply that these are the only good locations, but they are recommended for good birding plus accessibility and convenience. A majority are public areas without fees. Of the private areas, some are owned by non-profit concerns and can be visited by permission or for a fee.

The same general format is followed for each entry. To help users get oriented, the county and state of each location are listed, along with the number of the location map on which the described area can be found; if more than one map is listed, the first number corresponds to the most detailed map.

The first paragraph, **Attractions**, briefly states why a birder would go there. Next are **Directions** for reaching each location by automobile. The directions are brief and the aid of a road map of the greater St. Louis area is suggested. Adequate maps are available at most convenience stores and service stations and one of the best for the city and portions of surrounding counties can be obtained from the American Automobile

Association (AAA). Directions usually begin from the St. Louis metropolitan area (within the I-255/I-270 loop) and proceed along one of the major exit routes (Interstate or U. S. highways).

Next comes a general **Description** of the area, including its size and the habitats it contains. **Best Sites** describes in greater detail the specific places where birding has been most successful. Such sites, of course, can change from year to year, but the ones mentioned have historically been the most productive. The sites are usually listed sequentially, as the birder might proceed from one to another in the course of a birding trip.

The **Birds** section offers an outline of what species can be expected at the location throughout the year, including breeding birds and migrants. It does not list all species that have been seen in the area, but focuses on the less common species and those species characteristic of the area that might be reliably found there. In some cases rare and uncommon species that have been seen in the past are mentioned in order to show the birding potential.

The last item included in each entry is **General Information**, which includes information about toilet facilities, accommodations, and other services. It also indicates when the area is open or closed (e.g., for hunting) or any other specific restrictions one might not anticipate.

Common Nighthawk

Locations in the city and county of St. Louis, Missouri, are described first. These are followed by locations in adjacent St. Charles County, more distant Missouri locations, and finally by Illinois birding locations. Each major location is given a code letter which is keyed to the maps. For example, **[K]** refers to the Busch Conservation Area, which is shown on map 9. Some specific sites within some large birding locations are additionally given number designations; for example, **[K-6]** refers to Lake 33, which lies within the Busch Conservation Area.

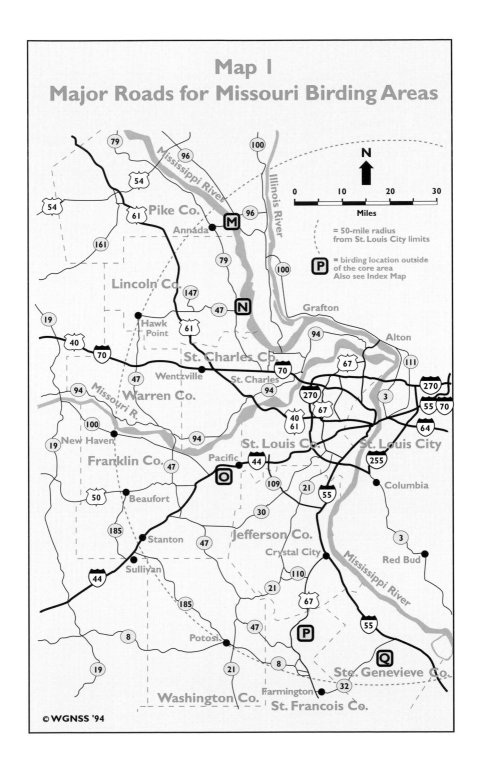

Map 1
Major Roads for Missouri Birding Areas

N

| 0 | 10 | 20 | 30 |
Miles

= 50-mile radius
from St. Louis City limits

P = birding location outside
of the core area
Also see Index Map

79
96
100
54
Mississippi River
Illinois River
54
Pike Co.
61
M
96
Annada
161
79
100
Lincoln Co.
147
Grafton
19
47
N
Hawk
Point
61
94
Alton
40
St. Charles Co.
67
111
70
47
Wentzville
St. Charles
270
94
94
Warren Co.
70
270
Missouri R.
270
3
55 70
100
40
67
New Haven
61
64
19
94
St. Louis Co.
St. Louis City
Franklin Co.
Pacific
44
255
O
109
Columbia
50
Beaufort
21
55
30
185
Jefferson Co.
Stanton
47
Crystal City
3
44
110
Red Bud
Sullivan
Mississippi River
21
185
67
8
47
55
19
P
Potosi
21
8
Q
Ste. Genevieve Co.
Washington Co.
Farmington
32
St. Francois Co.

© WGNSS '94

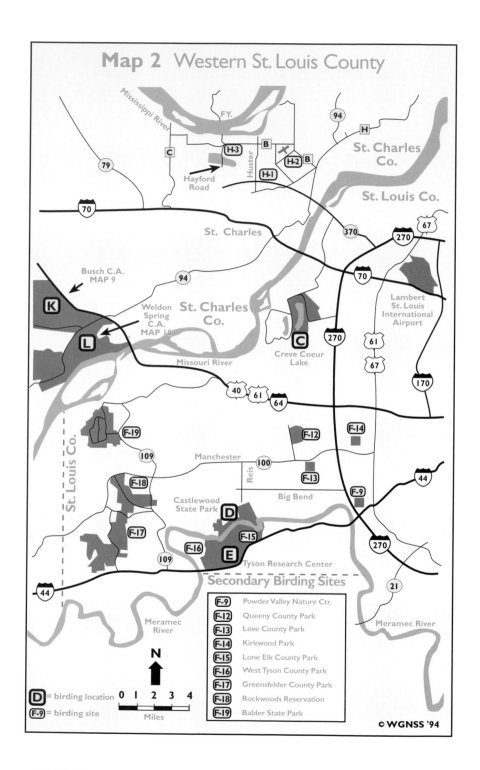

Map 2 Western St. Louis County

Mississippi River

FY.

94

H

C

H-3

B

Huster

H-2

B

St. Charles
Co.

Hayford
Road

H-1

70

St. Louis Co.

79

St. Charles

370

270

67

Busch C.A.
MAP 9

94

70

K

Weldon
Spring
C.A.
MAP 10

St. Charles
Co.

Lambert
St. Louis
International
Airport

L

61

Missouri River

Creve Coeur
Lake

C

270

67

St. Louis Co.

40

61

64

F-14

170

F-12

F-19

109

Manchester

100

44

F-18

Reis

F-13

F-9

Castlewood
State Park

D

Big Bend

270

F-17

F-15

F-16

E

109

Tyson Research Center

21

44

Secondary Birding Sites

Meramec
River

Meramec River

N

F-9	Powder Valley Nature Ctr.
F-12	Queeny County Park
F-13	Love County Park
F-14	Kirkwood Park
F-15	Lone Elk County Park
F-16	West Tyson County Park
F-17	Greensfelder County Park
F-18	Rockwoods Reservation
F-19	Babler State Park

D = birding location   0 1 2 3 4

F-9 = birding site   Miles

© WGNSS '94

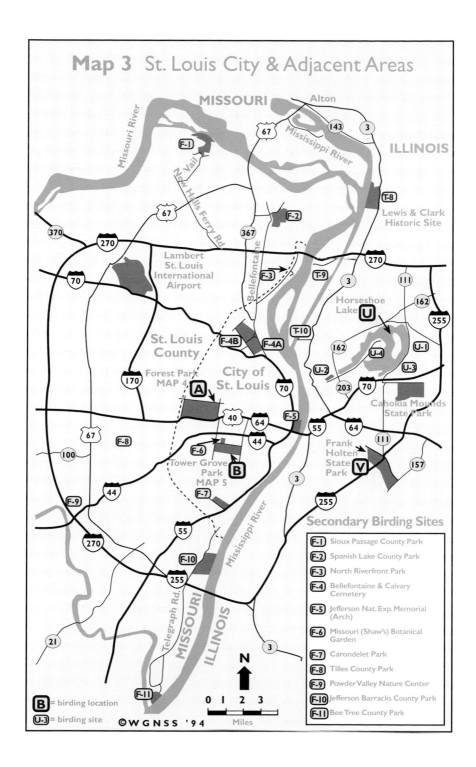

Map 3 St. Louis City & Adjacent Areas

MISSOURI

Alton

ILLINOIS

Missouri River

Mississippi River

New Halls Ferry Rd

F-1

F-2

Lewis & Clark
Historic Site

T-8

Lambert
St. Louis
International
Airport

Bellefontaine

F-3

T-9

T-10

Horseshoe
Lake U

St. Louis
County

F-4B   F-4A

City of
St. Louis

U-4

U-2

U-1

U-3

Cahokia Mounds
State Park

Forest Park
MAP 4

A

Tower Grove
Park
MAP 5

B

F-6

F-5

F-8

Frank
Holten
State
Park V

F-7

F-9

F-10

Mississippi River

Telegraph Rd.

MISSOURI

ILLINOIS

N

B = birding location
U-3 = birding site   ©WGNSS '94

0 1 2 3
Miles

Secondary Birding Sites

F-1 Sioux Passage County Park

F-2 Spanish Lake County Park

F-3 North Riverfront Park

F-4 Bellefontaine & Calvary
Cemetery

F-5 Jefferson Nat. Exp. Memorial
(Arch)

F-6 Missouri (Shaw's) Botanical
Garden

F-7 Carondelet Park

F-8 Tilles County Park

F-9 Powder Valley Nature Center

F-10 Jefferson Barracks County Park

F-11 Bee Tree County Park

IF YOU ONLY HAVE A DAY . . .

If you are a visitor to St. Louis and you only have a short time to go birding, here are the best and most convenient birding locations.

If it's spring or early summer and you want to see the breeding warblers and other passerines of the Ozarks, visit the *Busch* **[K]** and *Weldon Spring* **[L]** *Conservation Areas* or *Shaw Arboretum* **[O]**. Each of these areas requires several hours to bird thoroughly. Shaw Arboretum and Weldon Spring must be birded on foot, but Busch can be birded by car. Each of these areas is a 45-minute drive (west) from downtown. The Busch Conservation Area is probably the best single location for seeing a large diversity of species any time of year.

If it's spring or fall and you want to observe the songbird migration, *Tower Grove Park* **[B]** is the best place.

If you are interested in water birds like herons and egrets (summer), ducks (fall and early spring), or gulls (late fall through early spring), try *Horseshoe Lake* **[U]**, which is quickly reached from downtown, or the *Riverlands Environmental Demonstration Area* **[G]**, which is about a 35-minute drive (north) from downtown.

If it is the middle of winter and you want to see large concentrations of Bald Eagles or gulls, *Riverlands* **[G]** is the most convenient location.

Finally, if you want to find a Eurasian Tree Sparrow, read the discussion of this species at the end of the **SPECIES ACCOUNTS,** and good luck!

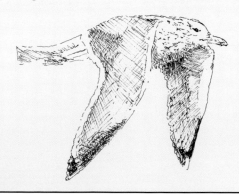

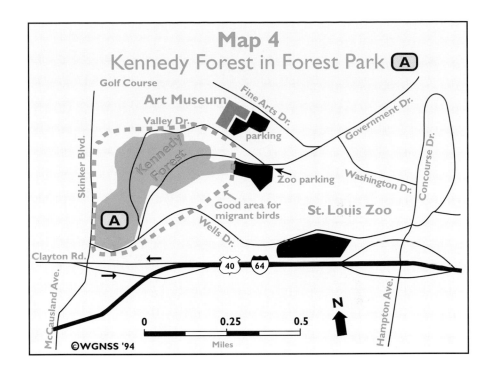

JOHN F. KENNEDY FOREST IN FOREST PARK   [A]
St. Louis, Missouri   *(Maps 4 & 3)*

Attractions: Because the Kennedy Forest is one of the few tracts of dense woodland in the city of St. Louis, it is an outstanding migrant trap for songbirds and other birds.

Directions: From US-40/I-64, take the Forest Park exit (Hampton Avenue) and turn north for 0.2 miles, passing the zoo. Turn left from Concourse Drive onto Washington Drive for 0.3 miles (along the edge of the zoo); turn left onto Government Drive for 0.3 miles, and park near a rustic stairway entrance on the right leading into the forest at the east end. Alternatively, turn right from Government Drive onto Fine Arts Drive or Valley Drive to the parking lot adjacent to the Art Museum. Cross the grass field, south of the museum, to enter the east end of Kennedy Forest.

Description and Best Sites: Forest Park (nearly 1,300 acres) is located on the western edge of the city of St. Louis. The John F. Kennedy Memorial Forest occupies the southwest corner of the park, west of the St. Louis Zoo and south of the St. Louis Art Museum. The Kennedy Forest, which was spared from the woodcutter's ax when Forest Park was the site of the World's Fair in 1904, is about 50 acres in size and one of the best places to observe migrant songbirds in the St. Louis area. Songbirds migrate mostly at night. When the sun comes up, they seek a place to feed and rest. The Kennedy Forest stands out like a green island in a concrete sea and attracts and concentrates high-flying birds from a wide area. On spring mornings, the density of migrants in the Kennedy Forest is much greater than that of forests in rural areas. Species that feed in treetops flit about from one large oak to another, while species that feed in the lower canopy and near the ground are attracted by the dense underbrush. Many foot trails lead through the forest, and a bike path parallels Valley Drive. Birding is good in the forest on both sides of Valley Drive and Government Drive as well as along the entire perimeter of the forest.

Birds: The best time to visit is during the spring migration in late April and early May, although large numbers of fall migrants have been observed in late August and September. During the spring migration, more than 30 warbler species and most of the eastern flycatchers, thrushes, vireos, tanagers, and orioles are seen. Resident birds include Great Horned Owl and several species of woodpecker. Making multiple rounds between 7 and 11 a.m. increases the chance of seeing a wide variety of species, but even short visits can be productive during peak migration periods. Sometimes migrant herons, hawks, and nightjars spend the night in the forest and are spotted by early birders.

General Information:
Forest Park is an urban park that is used by many people for many purposes. This is of little consequence to the birds but can be a source of irritation for birders. People in the forest without binoculars are probably not birders, and birding with one or more

entrance to nature trail

companions is suggested. Watch for bicycle traffic on the bike paths and car traffic on Valley Drive and Government Drive. At this writing, most of the foot trails and bridges are in poor repair, but plans exist for renovation and management by the Missouri Department of Conservation; some roads in the forest may be closed in the future. Restrooms are available just inside the rear entrance to the Art Museum.

The St. Louis Audubon Society has regularly scheduled bird walks in the Kennedy Forest, starting behind the Art Museum between 7:30 and 8:00 a.m. on weekends at the end of April and beginning of May. These walks are free and open to the public. Contact St. Louis Audubon at (314) 822-6595 for details.

In addition to the Kennedy Forest, Forest Park also has large fields, savannahs, several golf courses, and numerous lagoons that attract a few migrant waterfowl. Moreover, the park contains the St. Louis Art Museum, Jefferson Memorial Historical Museum, Jewel Box Gardens, St. Louis Science Center, Municipal Theater, and St. Louis Zoological Garden. The zoo includes a large collection of birds (mostly foreign) in several outdoor cages, on two waterfowl lakes, and in the bird house, which contains numerous natural habitat exhibits without glass walls. The bird flight cage has an elevated visitor walkway winding through its 227-foot length.

bird flight cage

TOWER GROVE PARK [B]

St. Louis, Missouri (Maps 5 & 3)

Attractions: Tower Grove Park is the most popular location in the area for viewing migrant passerines. It is centrally located and a place to see a wide variety of birds easily in a short amount of time.

Directions: Take I-44 (or I-64/US-40) to the Kingshighway exit. Go south on Kingshighway to Magnolia Avenue, approximately 0.5 miles south of I-44. Turn left onto Magnolia Avenue, and park on the right side of the street, about a block east from Kingshighway. Enter the park anywhere along the street. Here, you are close to the Gaddy Wild Bird Garden described below.

Some birders will want to continue east on Magnolia Avenue to Tower Grove Drive. Make a right turn into the park, and then make another right turn immediately. Drive past the tennis court area and horse stables; park just past these two landmarks. The best birding area in the park is the northwest corner, near the corner of Magnolia Avenue and Kingshighway.

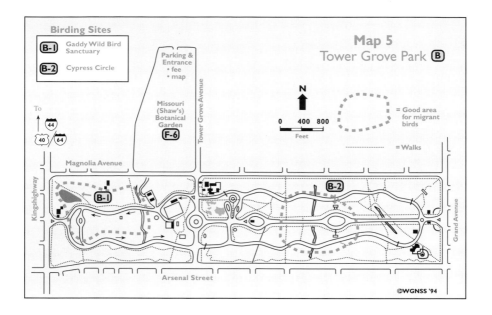

Description and Best Sites: Tower Grove Park (about 270 acres in size) is an old Victorian park that is 1.4 miles in length but only a few blocks in width. Like Forest Park, Tower Grove Park is a migrant trap. Most of the park area consists of old trees with no understory (savannah). Local birders usually walk the area from the horse stables west to the bushes and trees bordering the lone house on Magnolia Avenue, then continue west to the "brushpile", the previous site of an unattractive pile of tree trimmings with an amazing ability to attract interesting birds. The brushpile no longer exists, as the area was converted into a bird garden, the *Robert and Martha Gaddy Wild Bird Garden* **[B-1]**, by Webster Groves Nature Study Society, Missouri Department of Conservation, and Tower Grove Park. (Local birders often still call it "the brushpile," however.) The garden now offers a supply of dripping water, plantings attractive to birds, and a bark-chip footpath. After checking this area and the adjacent small pine grove, cross the park road to the south in order to investigate the holly trees before meandering back to the horse stables. Successive rounds usually produce birds not seen on the first trip. The park is worth checking mornings and evenings during the spring and fall migrations.

Another good birding spot is located on the central east-west drive, one-quarter mile west of the Grand Avenue entrance at *cypress tree circle* **[B-2]**. The circle and the nearby small creek to the west provide good viewing of birds. Even when the leaves have fully opened on the deciduous trees, the cypress trees have ample "windows" to see the birds.

Birds: During the spring and fall migration, a visit to Tower Grove park offers a quick, concentrated snapshot of the migration of songbirds through the St. Louis area. This means that a given day may be dull and slow, jumping with activity, or anything in between, according to the weather and the number of migrants. It also means that in the course of a season, Tower Grove Park hosts virtually all of the flycatchers, kinglets, thrushes, vireos, warblers, tanagers, and orioles, and many of the finches and sparrows, that pass through St. Louis. Some uncommon species seem to be found in the park more regularly than anywhere else in the area; outstanding examples are the Yellow-bellied Flycatcher, Connecticut and Black-throated Blue Warblers, and Clay-colored Sparrow. There have also been several records of out-of-habitat birds that used the park as a handy stopover (e.g., Virginia Rail and Le Conte's Sparrow). For ease of finding, viewing, and following migrant passerines, Tower Grove Park is the best location in the area.

There are, of course, some year-round resident birds like Carolina Chickadee, Tufted Titmouse, several woodpeckers, Northern Cardinal, House Finch, and Eastern Screech-Owl (check south-facing tree holes). However, it is migration that lures birders here, from March through late May (or even the first few days of June) and again from early or mid August into November. In addition to trees and shrubs, the skies should be scanned for swallows, nighthawks, and the occasional heron or raptor; Mississippi Kites, accipiters, and falcons have been sighted a number of times.

General Information: Although it is an urban park, most birders feel comfortable birding in Tower Grove Park alone. Restrooms are available near the tennis courts, and there are plenty of picnic tables in the area.

CREVE COEUR LAKE AND
LITTLE CREVE COEUR LAKE   [C]
St. Louis County, Missouri   *(Maps 6 & 2)*

Attractions: Creve Coeur Lake and the surrounding wooded park attracts water birds and migrating songbirds. Little Creve Coeur Lake is a transient spring wetland area that attracts marsh birds. Both areas are easily reached from Lambert St. Louis International Airport.

Directions: Located west of I-270 in central St. Louis County, the lake can be reached by exiting west from I-270 at Exit 17 (Dorsett Road), which is about 5 miles north of US-40/I-64, or 3 miles south of the I-70 junction with I-270. Proceed west on Dorsett Road approximately 1.5 miles to Marine Avenue. Turn right, and drive down winding Marine Avenue for 0.4 miles to the lake and boat launch ramps on the left.

Description: Creve Coeur Lake is a shallow oxbow of the Missouri River and the only natural lake in St. Louis County. It is almost two miles in length and is fed by Creve Coeur Creek. Prior to construction of the levees along the Missouri River (less than 2 miles away), the lake was routinely subject to flooding. During this earlier period shorebird habitat was available, though unpredictable. The lake, which is located in Creve Coeur County Park, has now been dredged and manicured to include an artificial beach. Bluffs border the southeast side and flat farmlands skirt the northwest side of the lake. Extensive open woods with occasional dense undergrowth cover the bluffs. The sand beach parallels Marine Avenue on the northeast side of the lake. The "improvements" have led to increased park use on weekends, which in turn has caused birding opportunities to decrease.

Best Sites: The *open woods on top of the bluff* can be accessed along a road with many loops through the main picnic and ballfield areas of the park. Turn right off Dorsett Road at the park entrance sign just before Marine Avenue.

Greensfelder Memorial, also on top of the bluff, provides a lake overlook. Adjacent woods along the bluff can provide opportunities for eye-level observation of migrants in treetops. At the end of Dorsett Road, turn right onto Marine Avenue; the entrance is just ahead on the left.

The *waterfall* can be reached by returning to Marine Avenue, turning left, and proceeding to the bottom of the bluff. Turn left into the parking lot and continue to the far end. A trail follows along the bottom of the bluff.

Fisherman's Point is reached by a gravel park road on the northwest side of the lake. Follow Marine Avenue to the junction with Creve Coeur Mill Road. Turn left, take the first park road to the left after crossing the railroad tracks (approximately 1.4 miles), and follow the gravel road to the point (0.4 miles).

Little Creve Coeur Lake is located west of Creve Coeur Lake. The "lake" only contains water following wet weather or after the spring thaw; it is usually dry by summer, and some years it doesn't exist at all. When water is available in spring, it is a good birding area for shorebirds and waterfowl. It is reached by following Creve Coeur Mill Road for an additional 1.6 miles (beyond the road to Fisherman's Point) to St. Louis County Waterworks Road. Turn right, go 0.4 miles to River Valley Road, and turn right. Enter the Creve Coeur Athletic Complex and park in the parking lot; the lake is behind the complex. Check surrounding fields and bushes for sparrows and other small passerines, including the Eurasian Tree Sparrow.

Birds: The wooded bluffs of the park are good for migrant warblers and other passerines. Some traditional residents, such as Prothonotary or Worm-eating Warblers, are now difficult to find since the park is so well maintained, but Louisiana Waterthrush can still be found in the spring at the waterfall. The lake often hosts ducks, grebes, terns, and loons during migration, but one must bird early before other park activities commence. The fields along the access road to Fisherman's Point sometimes contain Bobolinks, Grasshopper Sparrows, and Dickcissels in the spring.

General Information: Heavy use of the park for boating, picnicking, and other activities has discouraged local birders from regularly covering the area; this is especially true on weekends and holidays. The visiting birder might do well, however, on a weekday or early in the morning, especially in spring and fall. Restrooms are available throughout the northeast side of the park.

CASTLEWOOD STATE PARK [D]
St. Louis County, Missouri *(Map 2)*

Attractions: Castlewood State Park offers good birding opportunities for several species of breeding passerines, particularly species of riparian forests.

Directions: The park is located in west St. Louis County. Take I-270 (west of the city) to Big Bend Road (about 2.3 miles south of Manchester Road). Go west on Big Bend Road, which becomes Oak Street, for six miles to Ries Road. Turn left onto Ries Road and follow it to the park entrance. Turn left at the entrance sign and continue on the park road to the parking lot just past the railroad overpass.

Description: Castlewood State Park encompasses 1,778 acres straddling both sides of the Meramec River. The park contains a wide variety of natural habitats, including a small stream valley, floodplain, gravel bars, and the Meramec River. The primary lowland forest trees include silver maple, box elder, black elder, black willow, white ash, and sycamore. The uplands are forested with elm, white oak, northern red oak, shagbark hickory, and redbud. Fourteen miles of trails wind through the park, including the three-mile River Trail.

Best Sites: The scenic *River Trail* offers the best view of the river and of the riparian birds. The three-mile *Grotpeter Trail* winds through the park's uplands and provides a panoramic view of the bottomland forests and the river.

Birds: From the bottomland woods, Acadian Flycatchers can be heard, as well as White-eyed and Yellow-throated Vireos. Castlewood Park is a good location for seeing the Cerulean, Yellow-throated, and Prothonotary Warblers. These riparian birds are sometimes seen and heard at eye level. This stretch of the Meramec River is also a good spot to hear and see Fish Crows. The river also offers Belted Kingfisher and swallows. Woodpeckers, including the Pileated Woodpecker, frequent the bottomlands. The woods accommodate cuckoos, owls, warblers, and tanagers.

General Information: Castlewood State Park is open from 7 a.m. to 9 p.m. from April 1 through October 31 and from 7 a.m. to 6 p.m. the remainder of the year. Camping is not allowed in the park. Insect repellent is advisable. Pit toilets are located near the parking lot. The telephone number is (314) 527-6481.

TYSON RESEARCH CENTER [E]
St. Louis County, Missouri   *(Map 2)*

Attractions: The Tyson Research Center of Washington University is a good area for general birding and for finding certain specialty species of the Ozark forests that are hard to find elsewhere.

   Note: Although Tyson is birder friendly, access is by permission only; see **General Information**. At this writing the future status of Tyson is uncertain and access by birders and the general public may become unobtainable.

Directions: Take I-44 west about 7 miles from the I-44/I-270 junction in southwest St. Louis County to the Antire Road/Beaumont exit. The entrance gate is on the right at the end of the exit ramp.

Description: Tyson is a 2,000-acre tract of oak-hickory forest and old fields with ponds, springs, caves, and other karst features. A former army munitions storage facility, it serves its parent institution and other St. Louis academic institutions as a site for research and education. To serve the St. Louis community further, it provides a home for the Wolf Sanctuary, World Bird Sanctuary, and Wildlife Assistance, Inc. *These* *enterprises are not to be visited or approached by guests of Tyson except by specific arrangements made in advance.*

Best Sites: There are many trails, both on top of the ridges and along the Meramec River. Bird feeders are maintained at the gatehouse, headquarters, and photo blind. Hummingbird feeders are present in season. A vulture feeder attracts raptors, crows, and mammalian scavengers. On the south side of I-44, across the overpass from the entrance, is an excellent spot to watch the fall hawk migration.

Broad-winged Hawk

Birds: Tyson is a good place for finding resident birds of oak-hickory forest: Wild Turkey (abundant), all resident woodpeckers, Carolina Wren, Eastern Bluebird, Barred and Great Horned Owls, and hawks (including Red-shouldered). Breeding species include warblers (Prothonotary, Cerulean, Northern Parula, Yellow-throated, Blue-winged, Worm-eating, Yellow-breasted Chat, and Ovenbird), vireos (Warbling, Red-eyed, Yellow-throated, and White-eyed), both tanagers, both orioles, Rose-breasted Grosbeak, Whip-poor-will, occasionally Chuck-will's-widow, flycatchers (including Acadian), Bewick's Wren (scarce, but almost regular), and American Woodcock. Many migrants also visit the area, including Mississippi Kites. Winter visitors include Purple Finch, Pine Siskin, and Evening Grosbeak (some years only).

Research activities have included semi-annual bird censuses and studies of the impact of insect-eating birds on the consumption of plants by insects.

General Information: The Tyson gate is attended 8:00 a.m. to 6:00 p.m. and 7:00 p.m. to 11:30 p.m., seven days per week, University holidays excepted. *Unexpected visitors are not admitted to the site, which is not open to the public.* To arrange a visit, birders should call the Tyson office (314-935-8430) during business hours (weekdays 8:00 to 4:30). With advance notice (one business day is suggested), the office can advise the gateman to admit you and provide a map, bird list, tick repellent, and summary of do's and don'ts. Some portions of the landscape are off limits. Upon request, the gateman can lend you a key to a gate in Tyson's north fence that opens onto the Chubb Trail, giving access to the Meramec River and its floodplain. The Webster Groves Nature Study Society sponsors at least one field trip to Tyson each year, usually in spring.

Between mid-April and early October, ticks abound in the landscape. The use of free and (if used in adequate amount) effective repellent (Permanone) applied to clothing is strongly urged! Toilet facilities are available at the gatehouse and headquarters. Information about The Friends of Tyson, an information, communication, and support

bunker at TRC

group, is available at Tyson's gatehouse, where one can also buy birdseed, honey, books, and checklists, or merely relax by the fire.

SECONDARY BIRDING SITES [F]
St. Louis city and St. Louis County *(Maps 2 & 3)*

Attractions: The following birding sites are scattered throughout the more developed parts of our area. Most provide pockets of wooded or open habitat that are used primarily by birders that live near them. While each offers a selection (sometimes limited) of summer and winter resident birds, it is during migration that these locations are often most productive, since migrants can turn up anywhere. Directions are general, with the interstate highways as points of reference. The sites are arranged from north to south. Most are urban and suburban parks that have picnic areas and toilet facilities, but only Babler State Park offers camping.

Best Sites: *Sioux Passage County Park* **[F-1].** In north St. Louis County, take I-270 and exit at New Halls Ferry Road. Drive north on New Halls Ferry Road about 4.3 miles to Vaile Road. Turn right onto Vaile Road to the junction with Old Jamestown Road. From there, turn left, and follow the well-marked signs to the park. This 188-acre park, bordering the Missouri River, is a mixture of upland woods, open fields, and riverbottom forest; it is crowded on weekends. Eurasian Tree Sparrows are regular here.

Spanish Lake County Park **[F-2].** The 320-acre park contains three lakes and is located in north St. Louis County. Take I-270 to Bellefontaine Road. Go north on Bellefontaine Road to Spanish Pond Road. Turn right and follow the road until you reach any of the three park entrances. Although wooded areas of the park are the size of the Kennedy Forest in Forest Park and some of the park is similar in quality, it is only birded by a few local birders. Spanish Lake, which has a 1.4-mile paved path around the edge that is wheelchair accessible, is rarely frozen and used by waterfowl in winter.

North Riverfront Park **[F-3]**. From the I-270 loop heading east, north of the city, take the last exit in Missouri (Riverview Boulevard), and go south less than one mile to the entrance and parking lots near the river. In winter, this Mississippi riverside park at Chain of Rocks (see also **[T-9]**) is a good place to observe waterfowl, gulls, Bald Eagles, and Eurasian Tree Sparrows. In spring, migrants can be heard singing along the tree-lined walking path and adjacent tree-covered hillsides. The park is best birded in the afternoon in order to have the sun behind you.

Bellefontaine **[F-4A]** and *Calvary Cemeteries* **[F-4B]**. In north St. Louis, exit I-70 at Kingshighway, and turn northeast (right if coming from the downtown area). After 0.8 miles, turn right onto West Florissant Avenue, and left shortly at the entrance of Bellefontaine Cemetery. The entrance to Calvary Cemetery is just north of the Bellefontaine Cemetery entrance on West Florissant at Calvary Avenue. These old cemeteries are on a high bluff. About 1,000 acres of mature trees and fields provide excellent habitat for winter finches and other passerines.

Jefferson National Expansion Memorial **[F-5]**. This tree-lined park, administered by the National Park Service, is located in downtown St. Louis on the riverfront, south of the historic Eades bridge. Out-of-town birders will want to visit the Gateway Arch, the nation's tallest monument, which provides a fine view to the east and west. The underground museum has an exceptional historical exhibit of the Lewis and Clark expedition. Not presently noted for its bird life, the Arch grounds should become a better birding site in the future as trees planted in the 1970's increase in size.

Missouri Botanical Garden ("Shaw's Garden") **[F-6]**. From eastbound I-64/US-40 or I-44 go south on Kingshighway to the stoplight at Southwest Avenue. Turn left and proceed to the next stoplight at Shaw Avenue. Turn right and follow the signs to the entrance and parking lots on the right. From downtown, take I-44 to the Vandeventer exit and follow the signs. The Garden has a nominal entrance fee, but it has free admission on Wednesday and Saturday until noon. The Climatron and the English and Japanese Gardens are the highlights of a visit. Purple Martins are regular in summer. Most local birders also like to visit *Tower Grove Park* (see location **[B]**), just south of the Garden. A booklet on the Garden's birds can be purchased in the bookstore, which also has many books on other nature-related topics.

Carondelet Park **[F-7]**. From downtown, take I-55 south. Exit at Loughborough, and go west to the park entrance. Located in the extreme south of the city of St. Louis, this 150-acre park has two modest lakes and is surrounded by mostly mature upland savannah forest.

Rosalie Tilles County Park **[F-8]**. Take I-64/US-40 to the McKnight Road exit (about one mile west of the I-170 exit). Go south on McKnight about 0.7 miles. This 66-acre park is located at McKnight and Litzsinger Roads. It consists of mostly mature savannah uplands, with one modest lake for waterfowl. Nearby large residences enhance the oasis effect of this small park.

Powder Valley Nature Center **[F-9]** (Missouri Department of Conservation). From downtown, take I-44 to the Lindbergh Boulevard exit. Take Lindbergh south 0.2 miles to Watson Road. Turn right onto Watson and continue for 0.5 miles to Geyer Road. Turn right onto Geyer Road and go 0.2 miles, crossing over I-44, and turn left at Cragwold Road, which leads to the entrance. The Nature Center office is open from 8 a.m. to 6 p.m. Tuesday through Sunday, year round. Inside, there are excellent nature displays and outside, there are numerous feeders in winter. This 120-acre upland forest has three trails; one is wheelchair accessible.

Jefferson Barracks County Park **[F-10]**. In south St. Louis County, exit I-255 at Telegraph Road and turn north (left if coming from Missouri). Drive north on Telegraph Road about 1.5 miles to the park entrance. Located on the Mississippi River, this 425-acre park is renowned for its military history. The habitat is mostly mature forest edges and open fields. *Sylvan Spring County Park* and the large Jefferson National Cemetery are nearby and offer additional similar habitat.

Bee Tree County Park **[F-11]**. South of the city, take I-255 and exit at Telegraph Road. Drive south on Telegraph Road about 4.5 miles to Becker Road. Turn left onto Becker and continue to the park entrance. This 195-acre park is located in the extreme southern tip of St. Louis County on Finestown and Becker Roads, next to the Mississippi River. The park, which consists of mostly mature forests stretched along the river bluffs, can be excellent for spring migrants.

Edgar M. Queeny County Park **[F-12]**. From I-270 west of city, exit at Manchester Road. Drive west for 2.2 miles to Weidman Road. Turn right, and drive north about one mile to the park entrance on the right. With 569 acres, this is one of the largest St. Louis County parks. There are numerous trails and bridal paths. The habitat is mostly mature upland forest and open fields, with streams and a few small ponds. The park is surrounded by suburbs.

John Allen Love Memorial County Park **[F-13]**. Take I-270 to the Manchester Road exit. Drive west on Manchester to Mason Lane, about 0.2 miles west of Barrett Station Road. Turn left to the park entrance. With a dense forest bordering a creek, this 48-acre park is a favorite of local birders during migration.

Kirkwood Park **[F-14]**. Take I-270 to the Manchester Road exit and turn east. Drive approximately 1.8 miles to Geyer Road. Turn right, and continue one mile to the park entrance. This 100-acre park contains a lake and an open forest; the southwest edge has a creek with bordering undergrowth.

Lone Elk County Park **[F-15]**. In southwest St. Louis County, this 405-acre park is reached by taking the MO-141 exit off I-44, about 4 miles west of I-270. Take the North Outer Road west; signs to the park are stationed along the road. In conjunction with the World Raptor Project, the park has a display of raptors for the viewing public. The park also contains a herd of bison and elk.

West Tyson County Park **[F-16]**. Take I-44 west to the Lewis Road exit, about 9.7 miles west of the junction of I-44 and I-270. Turn right onto Lewis Road; the park entrance is ahead on the right. This 240-acre park, which offers good hiking, is west of both the Tyson Research Center and Lone Elk Park. Together, these three areas provide a long greenway of upland Ozark forest between I-44 and the Meramec River.

A. P. Greensfelder Memorial County Park **[F-17]**. Take I-44 west to the Allenton (Six Flags) exit, 15 miles from the junction of I-270 and I-44. The park is located along Allenton and Hencken Roads on 1,754 acres and has extensive trails in a woodland and riverbottom setting.

Rockwoods Reservation **[F-18]**. Take I-44 west to MO-109. Turn right, and drive north to the entrance. This 3,200-acre area is managed by the Missouri Department of Conservation and has several hiking trails through steep hills and narrow valleys of mostly oak and hickory forest. Creeks provide the only open water.

Edmund A. Babler Memorial State Park **[F-19]**. Take I-44 west to MO-109. Turn right, and drive north about 8 miles on MO-109 to county highway C. Follow the road signs to the park entrance (total of 10 miles from I-44). This 2,400-acre park is mostly deciduous forest, fields, and picnic areas and has over 10 miles of trails. The habitat, similar to Rockwoods, is good for woodland birds. The park is crowded on weekends.

General Information: A glance at a local map will reveal a number of other small- to medium-sized parks throughout the area. Many of these have some birding habitat and offer reasonable prospects for bird finding, especially in spring and fall. The areas listed above are included by virtue of their size or familiarity among local birders, but you are encouraged to explore others.

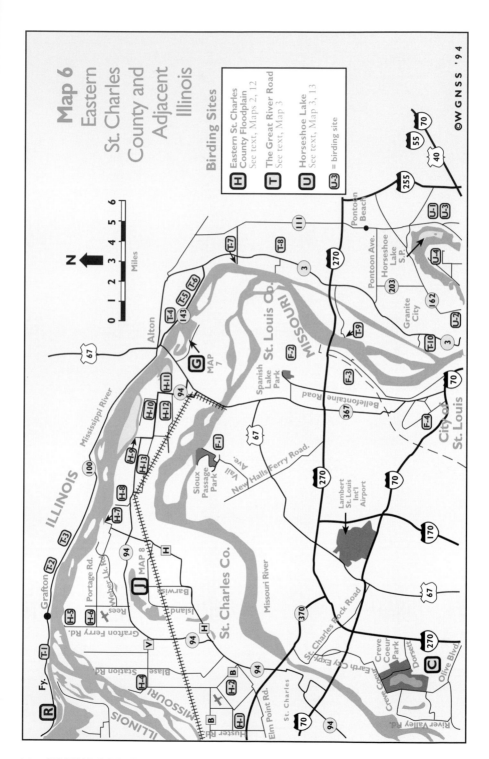

Map 6
Eastern
St. Charles
County and
Adjacent
Illinois

Birding Sites

[H] Eastern St. Charles
County Floodplain
See text, Maps 2, 12

[T] The Great River Road
See text, Map 3

[U] Horseshoe Lake
See text, Map 3, 13

[U-3] = birding site

©WGNSS '94

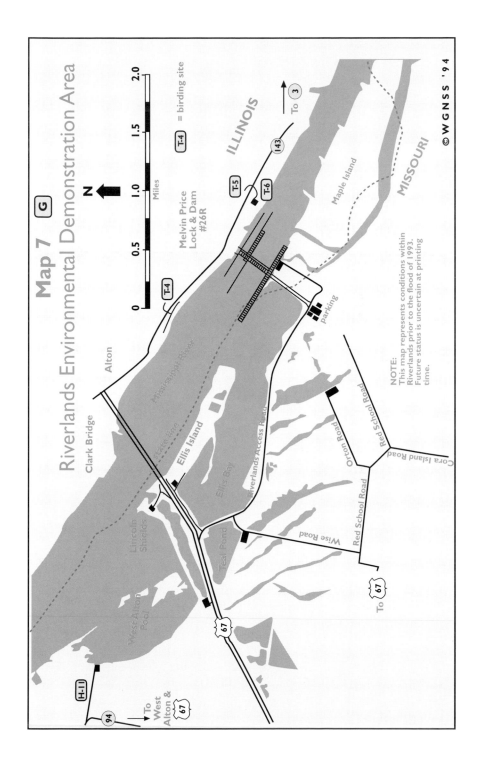

Map 7 G

Riverlands Environmental Demonstration Area

T-4 = birding site

N

Miles

0   0.5   1.0   1.5   2.0

Clark Bridge

Alton

ILLINOIS

MISSOURI

Melvin Price
Lock & Dam
#26R

Maple Island

To 3

143

T-5

T-6

T-4

Mississippi River

Levee line

Ellis Island

Ellis Bay

Lincoln
Shields

West Alton Pool

Teal Pond

Riverlands Access Road

parking

Orton Road

Red School Road

Cora Island Road

Wise Road

Red School Road

To 67

67

H-11

94

To
West
Alton &
67

NOTE:
This map represents conditions within
Riverlands prior to the flood of 1993.
Future status is uncertain at printing
time.

© WGNSS '94

RIVERLANDS ENVIRONMENTAL DEMONSTRATION AREA [G]

St. Charles County, Missouri *(Maps 7 & 6)*

Attractions: The Riverlands Environmental Demonstration Area is an outstanding area for birding the Mississippi River and associated wetlands. The area also contains extensive grasslands and marshes.

Directions: From I-270, drive north on MO-367, which becomes US-67 at Lindbergh Boulevard, and continue north over the Missouri River into St. Charles County. Proceed 2.5 miles past the junction of MO-94, turn right on the blacktop road, and proceed past the large service station to the entrance. If approaching from the north (Illinois), drive south from Alton over the Mississippi River on US-67. Turn left onto the blacktop road 0.3 miles from the Missouri end of the bridge, and proceed past the service station to enter Riverlands. A sign is on the right at the first junction. Access to this area may change in the future with completion of the new US-67 bridge over the Mississippi River and access roads.

Description: Riverlands was created by the U. S. Army Corps of Engineers in conjunction with the construction of the Melvin Price Locks and Dam (No. 26R). This largest of Mississippi River dams replaced the old Alton Dam

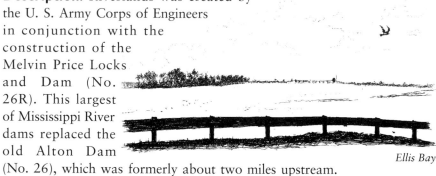

Ellis Bay

(No. 26), which was formerly about two miles upstream. An elevated access road on top of the dike divides the area into two main sections: on the north side of the road is the Ellis Bay waterfowl refuge and Ellis Island, while the area south of the road consists of prairie grasses and marshes. Birding stops along the main access road are described below.

Note: The flood of 1993 heavily damaged this area and, at this writing, the area is being restored.

Best Sites: *Ellis Bay*, which consists of 500 acres of lowland flooded by the new dam, can be viewed from the access road. Water levels in the bay are controlled by the dam. At normal river levels, the bay averages 5 feet in depth and includes a number of small islands and shallow areas. When high water volume is anticipated, the main gates of the dam are opened, drawing water from the bay and creating extensive mudflats.

To reach **Ellis Island**, turn left off the access road opposite the service station; follow the road a short distance, turn right onto the island, and proceed to the parking lot. Parking is not allowed along the road. Boat usage is forbidden in Ellis Bay from October 1 through March 31, as the bay is designated a waterfowl refuge during that period.

South of the access road is an area of native prairie restoration. As part of the 1,200-acre **prairie-marsh** complex, 800 acres of former agricultural lands were converted to native grasses such as big bluestem, switchgrass, and eastern gamagrass. Numerous marshes totaling 400 acres in area vary in size from 50 acres to small potholes and ditches with average depths of 18 inches.

Teal Pond is located directly behind the service station and is best viewed from the parking area to the east off Wise Road. Wise Road (currently gravel) is the first right turn off the access road. **Wise Road Marsh** is located on the left side of Wise Road, about 200 yards east of Teal Pond.

Two Pecan Tree Pond is located on the right side of the main access road 0.5 miles east of Wise Road. The pond is surrounded by 15 acres of native plants. Across the road is a sandy, weed-covered knoll that is a good place to find sparrows. A raptor hacking station is located just east of Two Pecan Tree Pond. Three Peregrine Falcons were successfully raised and released there in 1990, the project's first year. The station was also used for reintroduction of three Bald Eagles in 1992.

The next marsh east of the hacking box is called **Heron Pond** by birders. Flooding of the marshes is accomplished by controlling gravity drainage from the east end of the marsh complex. Further east on the access road is an observation tower.

The access road changes into a gravel road that ends at a parking lot just below the dam. This is a good place to watch gulls in winter, as the parking lot is close to the river and the sun is behind you.

Birds: Riverlands is probably the best location in the area for finding species from all the main groups of water-related birds (waterfowl, wading birds, shorebirds, marsh birds, gulls, terns, etc.). A wide variety of species can be expected, even though the habitat varies somewhat with the water level of the river and the total numbers of birds may not be as great as at some other locations. Since most viewing must be done from the access road, sometimes at considerable distance from the birds, a spotting scope is useful.

Loons, grebes and waterfowl (including over 20 species of ducks) occur during migration. Many birds stop on Ellis Bay, or farther out in the river channel, but a good number also rest on Teal Pond, where they can be viewed at closer range. Surface-feeding ducks fly in and out of the marshy sloughs in the prairie. Double-crested Cormorants are found in large numbers in spring, late summer, and fall; in August 1992 they were joined by a Neotropic Cormorant, the first recorded in the St. Louis area.

Shorebirds are prevalent when water levels are low enough to produce mudflats; Wise Road marsh usually yields the greatest variety. Two Pecan Tree Pond and Heron Pond can also be productive, and shorebirds can be viewed all along the shore of Ellis Bay from the access road if mud edges along the shore are exposed. The slough at Ellis Island should also be checked. In the first two years of its existence, 28 species of shorebirds were observed at Riverlands, the rarest of which were Piping Plover, Black-necked Stilt, American Avocet, Marbled Godwit, Ruddy Turnstone, Red Knot, and Red-necked Phalarope.

Pied-billed Grebes nest in Teal Pond. King Rail, Virginia Rail, Sora, and Common Moorhen have been seen in spring on the potholes east of the parking lot on Ellis Island. All of the regular herons and egrets can be seen from spring through fall; in particular, Snowy Egrets are more readily found here than anywhere else except Horseshoe Lake.

A variety of gulls has been observed at Riverlands. Ring-billed Gulls, usually the commonest species, are present almost year-round, but Herring Gulls will sometimes supplant the Ring-bills entirely during winter cold snaps. Other gull species seen here include Franklin's and Bonaparte's (both regular migrants), Thayer's and Glaucous (both scarce, but regular in winter), and several rarer species such as Great Black-backed, Lesser Black-backed, and Little. The first Ross's Gull to be seen in Missouri occurred here in late 1991 and early 1992. Migrant terns are seen primarily on Ellis Bay, with Forster's, Caspian, and Black the most regular species. A few jaegers have also been spotted.

Riverlands is probably the closest and most accessible place from St. Louis to see large numbers of Bald Eagles during the winter months. Other common winter raptors are Northern Harrier and Red-tailed Hawk. Rough-legged Hawks appear sporadically, and Short-eared Owls can be seen flying over the prairie area, usually after sundown. During migration, Ospreys and Peregrine Falcons may be seen.

Perching birds are less obvious, but many species have been noted. Horned Larks are common along the access road, sometimes accompanied by Lapland Longspurs in winter. All swallows, especially Tree, are seen during migration. Fish Crows are best observed in spring. Sedge Wrens are common in the prairie grasses in August, and Common Yellowthroat, Dickcissel, and Grasshopper Sparrow are breeding species. Finally, Riverlands is a good place to observe Eurasian Tree Sparrows, which occur in compact flocks in the taller weed patches.

General Information: Carefully obey all signs; the rules are enforced. Do not enter the marsh areas south of the access road without specific permission from the Corps ranger on patrol; usually permission must be obtained the previous day or earlier at Riverlands headquarters. Hunting is not permitted at Riverlands. Restrooms are available at the service station.

ST. CHARLES COUNTY FLOODPLAIN   [H]
St. Charles County, Missouri   *(Map 6)*

Attractions: The floodplain between the Mississippi and Missouri Rivers north of the St. Louis metropolitan area provides an extensive region of good habitat for open-country raptors and passerines, as well as riparian woodland species and sometimes shorebirds.

Directions: In northwest St. Louis County, take I-270 to the MO-370 exit. Go west on MO-370 into St. Charles County, and exit at Mueller Road. From here, the preferred birding route meanders, gradually heading east along MO-94 to US-67 for a total distance of 21 miles from MO-370. Some birders might prefer to first visit *Riverlands Environmental Demonstration Area* **[G]** and then wind their way west through the floodplains, reversing the order of the locations described under **Best Sites**.

Description: The floodplain of eastern St. Charles Co. is mostly open farm land. It also encompasses rural airports, private hunting clubs, river access points, bottomland forests, and a sewage lagoon. The marshes of *Marais Temps Clair* **[J]** lie at the center of the region.

Best Sites: For this region, the birding sites described here can be visited in the order presented to approximate a tour from west to east through the region. This route, in effect, is the Missouri equivalent of the *Great River Road* tour **[T]** described later for Illinois.

The *Mueller Road lagoon* **[H-1]** can be reached by taking MO-370 to the Mueller Road exit. Follow Mueller Road for one mile to the soccer fields on the left, which often contain Eastern Meadowlarks, Horned Larks, Killdeer, and other species in migration. The lagoon itself, at the northwest edge of the soccer fields, can be good for ducks and shorebirds, including Piping Plover. Look for a stairway and birders' platform near the fence.

To reach the *St. Charles Airport* **[H-2]** from Mueller Road, go past the lagoon, turn right onto Airport Road, and continue to county highway B. Turn left and proceed a short distance to a sharp bend to the left and continue for 0.3 miles to a small, unmarked pulloff on the left between two grass runways. Park here and discreetly check the runways (which are usually not in use). Upland Sandpipers, American Golden-Plovers, and Savannah and Grasshopper Sparrows are regular in migration. An especially lucky visit in late March or early April could turn up a Smith's Longspur.

From the airport, continue west on county highway B for 6.0 miles, passing over Dardenne Creek to

Upland Sandpiper

Hayford Road **[H-3]** on the left (see also maps 2 and 12). This road leads to fields that attract shorebirds if there is standing water. Be sure to stay on the road, as the adjacent land is private property. You must stop where a gate crosses the road; do not enter the duck-hunting club property beyond. Take care in turning around on this dead-end road; the edges can be soft.

From the junction of MO-94 and county highway B, drive 1.9 miles west on highway B to a sharp bend and go straight (north) on **Washeon Road [H-4]** to gain access to the Mississippi River. At the end of Washeon Road is a privately owned marina whose management is usually tolerant of birders. Check the river for waterfowl.

Starting again at the junction of MO-94 and county highway B and proceeding northeast, birders have the option of either continuing on MO-94 or exiting at county highway H to visit **Marais Temps Clair Conservation Area [J]**. If continuing on MO-94, drive one mile to the small Trinity Lutheran School. Across the road is a mudflat that can be productive during the shorebird migration.

Continue on MO-94 through the small town of Orchard Farm at a railroad crossing. Turn left onto **Grafton Ferry Road [H-5]** (1.2 miles from railroad crossing), checking the fields on both sides, past the **St. Charles County Airport [H-6]** (Smartt Field) all the way to the Mississippi River. Northern Harriers, Short-eared Owls, and Brewer's Blackbirds have been found in the fields. Barred Owls and passerines can be found in the woods near the river. The airfield itself is closed to the public, but sometimes birds may be seen by pausing along the boundary roads (especially Portage Road on the north side).

Northern Harrier

Return to MO-94, and turn left. Immediately past Rees Road, make a right turn into the north entrance of the **Marais Temps Clair Conservation Area [J]**. An area map is posted in the parking lot.

Continue east on MO-94 to county highway J. Turn left, and follow the markers through the town of *Portage Des Sioux* **[H-7]** to the shrine of Our Lady of the Rivers. The shrine extends into the Mississippi River and provides a good view of the river and its banks at any season.

For another access to the Mississippi River, continue east on MO-94 about 1.5 miles from the junction with county highway J to a road with a sign for the *Valley Sailing Association* **[H-8]**. This is a good spot for wintering waterfowl and gulls as well as wintering passerines in the tree-lined bottoms. Use caution when the gravel road is wet and soft.

Return to MO-94, turn left, and continue east for 3.5 miles to the entrance of the *Dresser Island Conservation Area* **[H-9]** on the left. Operated by the Missouri Department of Conservation, this river access has a six-mile hiking trail, circumnavigating the island along the Mississippi River. Even in the coldest winters, the water in the slough remains partly open because it is warmed by the effluent from the power plant upstream.

Green Heron

Return to MO-94. Turn left (east), and follow MO-94 for 1.7 miles to *Alta Villa Road* **[H-10]**. Turn left, and take the road to the river. Check the woods for passerines and owls. Turn left at the slough, and follow the road, checking for waterfowl. The water in the slough is often open in winter when other water has frozen.

Return to MO-94. Turn left (east), and drive less than a mile to the entrance of the *Harbor Point Yacht Club* **[H-11]**. Use caution when entering Harbor Point as MO-94 takes a sharp turn to the right at this intersection. This private marina discourages non-members from visiting. Nevertheless, the area on the left, before entering Harbor Point, can be productive for shorebirds and herons if mudflats are available. Continuing straight, past the Harbor Point marina entrance, the road dead-ends at an access to Alton Lake (West Alton Pool on Map 7).

Return to MO-94. Turn left (south) for 0.3 miles to *Saale Road* **[H-12]**. Turn right (west) on Saale Road for three miles to the farm on the left. This narrow property between the road and the Missouri River levee offers good potential for blackbirds and Eurasian Tree Sparrows. Continuing in the same direction on Saale Road, proceed to the junction with *Dwiggins Road* **[H-13]**, but be sure to check the fields along the way, especially any mudflats. Turn left onto Dwiggins Road and continue to MO-94, on which you turn right to complete the return loop eastward.

This is the end of the tour through the floodplain of eastern St. Charles County. Most birders will want to continue on MO-94 through West Alton where they will encounter US-67. Here, birders can decide to head north to visit *Riverlands Environmental Demonstration Area* **[G]** or to go south and return to St. Louis County.

Birds: The Missouri River has fewer birds to offer than the Mississippi, and the extensive plowed and planted fields harbor fewer birds than the occasional fallow fields or airport margins. The birder may drive past miles of apparent "desert" before coming across interesting single birds (such as hawks) or flocks (such as longspurs or blackbirds). Nevertheless, eastern St. Charles County has been the source of many records of rarities and many good days of ordinary birding. Below is a brief summary of additional species that regularly occur.

Any river access point may yield Great Blue Herons, Bald Eagles, and a variety of gulls and ducks (including rarities like the Oldsquaw) during migration and winter. The riverbanks are not a good place to seek shore-birds; these are usually seen in the fields following rains or flooding, or at the Mueller Road Lagoon or Marais Temps Clair. While many shorebird species are possible, the American Golden-Plover may be especially common in the early spring. Various raptors can be seen in the open country in winter, especially Northern Harriers, Red-tailed Hawks, Rough-legged Hawks (which vary from rare to fairly common, depending on the year), falcons (Prairie Falcon sightings have become almost regular), and Short-eared Owls. Passerine specialties are the ubiquitous Horned Lark, the Lapland Longspur that often accompany the larks in winter, the much scarcer but probably overlooked Smith's Longspur (in migration), and the occasional Western Meadowlark or Brewer's Blackbird. The mature woods along the rivers contain Barred Owls all year and lots of Wood Ducks and Prothonotary Warblers in the summer.

General Information: Unfortunately, MO-94 is a busy road. It has no shoulder and there is practically no place to pull off if a "good bird" is spotted. Stop-and-go birding is best done on the side roads. During periods of heavy rains, local flooding can occur on roads near the rivers. Many of these roads are gravel and can wash out in heavy flooding. *Do not drive through flood areas.* In the past, during major floods, parts of MO-94 have been under water, including all of West Alton. The *St. Louis Post-Dispatch* newspaper has detailed weather data with river stages (levels) referenced to "flood stages." Expect local flooding when river stages exceed flood stages by two or more feet for Grafton or Alton (the latter is listed as "Melvin Price tailwater" in the newspaper), since these levels influence the St. Charles County floodplain.

An annual Christmas Bird Count, centered at the town of Orchard Farm, includes most of the areas described here.

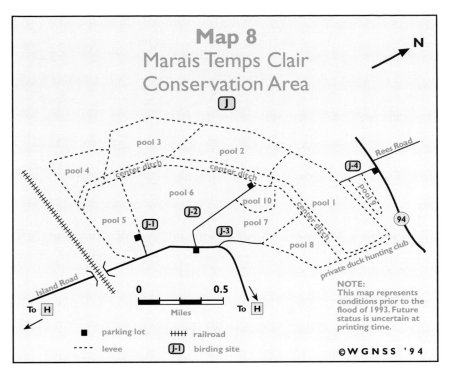

Map 8
Marais Temps Clair
Conservation Area
Ⓙ

N

pool 3

pool 2

Rees Road

pool 4

center ditch

center ditch

Ⓙ-4

pool 6

pool 10

pool 1

Ⓙ-2

Ⓙ-1

pool 5

Ⓙ-3

pool 7

94

pool 8

private duck hunting club

Island Road

0   0.5

To Ⓗ

Miles

To Ⓗ

NOTE:
This map represents
conditions prior to the
flood of 1993. Future
status is uncertain at
printing time.

■ parking lot   ┼┼┼┼ railroad

---- levee   Ⓙ-1 birding site

©WGNSS '94

MARAIS TEMPS CLAIR   [J]
St. Charles County, Missouri   *(Maps 8 & 6)*

Attractions: Marais Temps Clair is a large marsh accessible by gravel
roads surrounding maintained pools, with extensive fields (some
cultivated).

Directions: "MTC" is located northeast of St. Charles, Missouri. From
I-270, take MO-370 and cross the Missouri River. Take MO-94 north and
east to county highway H. There are four entrances to the Conservation
Area. The north entrance can be reached by continuing along MO-94
through Orchard Farm to a parking area on the right almost opposite Rees
Road (see **[H]**). The south entrances can be reached by taking county
highway H about 2 miles and turning left onto Island Road. The first south
entrance is on the left, just past the railroad overpass (approximately 3
miles from the intersection of MO-94 and county highway H); the second
and third come shortly thereafter, with the third located just before Island
Road turns to the right.

Description: Marais Temps Clair ("fair weather marsh") is a vestigial
oxbow lake located in the floodplain between the Mississippi and Missouri
Rivers. Most of the 920-acre Conservation Area was formerly a duck hunting

club that was purchased by the Missouri Department of Conservation as a wildlife area. The area has ten pools separated by levees, and water levels are maintained with pumps. The first south entrance has crops and native grasses growing on either side. Small stands of forest border much of the area.

Best Sites: From the *first south entrance* **[J-1]** and parking lot, walk the gravel levee road until it reaches another levee road. Head left along the levee to reach the shallow ends of pools 3, 4, and 5, which can be good for rails, bitterns, and wrens. From the *second south entrance* **[J-2]** road, drive to the small parking lot near a gate. This point is near the intersection of several pools (1, 2, 6, and 7) and the shorebird area (pool 10). The *third south entrance* **[J-3]** is a walk-in road that passes through forest before reaching the marsh; this section is good for owls and passerines.

From the *north entrance* **[J-4]** and parking lot along MO-94, walk the gravel road past a small pool and marsh on the left (pool 9) to the levee road along the north side of pools 1 and 2.

Birds: Marais Temps Clair offers year-round birding, although it is most attractive in late April and May. In winter, Snow Geese can be seen and in mild winters some ducks may also be present. Sparrows and finches can be flushed from the brushy fields. Northern Harriers feed over the marsh by day, and Short-eared Owls can sometimes be seen at dusk. The woods surrounding the marsh are a reliable place to find Great Horned and Barred Owls and Eastern Screech-Owls. In spring, grebes, bitterns, ducks, coots, rails, shorebirds, wrens, Bobolinks, and Yellow-headed Blackbirds are seen as migrants. Summer brings herons, plus nesting Least Bitterns, Willow Flycatcher, Common Yellowthroat, and Indigo Bunting. In fall, the marsh attracts ducks, shorebirds, sparrows, and blackbirds. Eurasian Tree Sparrows are

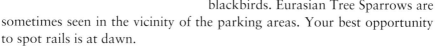

Red-winged Blackbirds

sometimes seen in the vicinity of the parking areas. Your best opportunity to spot rails is at dawn.

General Information: Marais Temps Clair is open throughout the year, but is closed to the public during the fall duck hunting season from dawn to 1:00 p.m. (check the Sunday *St. Louis Post-Dispatch* for dates). A spotting scope is needed to see shorebirds and waterfowl most effectively. Toilet facilities were destroyed in the flood of 1993.

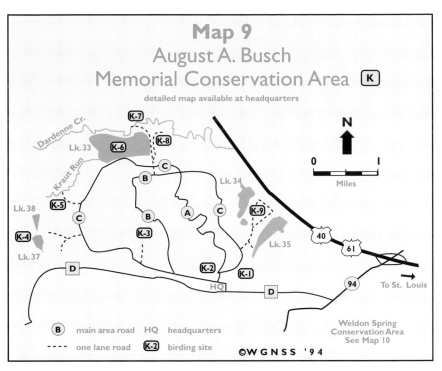

Map 9
August A. Busch
Memorial Conservation Area [K]

detailed map available at headquarters

Dardenne Cr.

K-7

K-8

Lk. 33

K-6

Kraut Run

C

B

Lk. 34

K-5

C

B

A

C

K-9

Lk. 38

Lk. 35

K-4

K-3

Lk. 37

K-2

D

K-1

HQ

D

94

To St. Louis

40

61

N

0   I

Miles

B   main area road   HQ   headquarters

---- one lane road   K-2   birding site

Weldon Spring
Conservation Area
See Map 10

©WGNSS '94

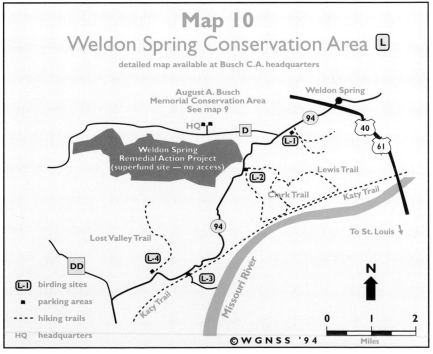

Map 10
Weldon Spring Conservation Area [L]

detailed map available at Busch C.A. headquarters

August A. Busch
Memorial Conservation Area
See map 9

Weldon Spring

HQ

94

40

D

L-1

61

Weldon Spring
Remedial Action Project
(superfund site — no access)

Lewis Trail

L-2

Clark Trail

Katy Trail

Lost Valley Trail

94

To St. Louis ↓

DD

L-4

Missouri River

L-3

Katy Trail

L-1   birding sites

■   parking areas

---- hiking trails

HQ   headquarters

N

0   I   2

Miles

©WGNSS '94

AUGUST A. BUSCH CONSERVATION AREA [K]
WELDON SPRING CONSERVATION AREA [L]
St. Charles County, Missouri   *(Maps 9, 10, & 2)*

Attractions: The Busch and Weldon Spring areas are large and easily accessible public places that offer considerable habitat diversity and the potential for a good bird list in any season (in early May, possibly 120 species in a day).

Directions: The two areas are located in St. Charles County near the junction of US-40/61 with MO-94. This junction is about 25 miles west of the St. Louis city limits, 15 miles west of the I-270 junction with US-40, and 12 miles southwest of St. Charles (junction of I-70 and MO-94).

To reach the entrance to the *Busch Conservation Area*, travel southwest on MO-94 for 1.1 miles from the junction of US-40/61. Turn right (west) at county highway D, continue 1.8 miles to the entrance signs, and then turn right into the headquarters and lodge parking areas. Detailed maps for both Conservation Areas and a bird checklist can be obtained from racks just inside the doorways to both the headquarters and lodge buildings or at the stop sign just inside the gate.

To reach *Weldon Spring Conservation Area*, travel south and west on MO-94, and turn off at any of the places listed under **Best Sites**.

Description: Busch Conservation Area (approximately 7,000 acres) is combined for this discussion with Weldon Spring Conservation Area (7,400 acres) because of their adjacent locations. Together these two areas take on an irregular shape that roughly spans a 6-mile by 6-mile region. Both areas are managed by the Missouri Department of Conservation. Because they are close to St. Louis, they get heavy usage, especially on weekends. Early morning birding is suggested.

Busch has a diversity of habitats that make it appealing to birds and birders throughout the year. There are more than 30 man-made lakes, numerous small ponds, sizable remnants of second-growth forests, pine groves, weedy fields, cultivated fields, creeks, modest marshy areas, and a sizable twin-pool shorebird area. The lakes vary in size from a few acres to almost 200 acres.

Weldon Spring has primarily two types of habitat, extensive open fields and sizable forest areas containing hiking trails. The southern edge of the area borders the Missouri River and includes a six-mile segment of the Missouri River Trail, or Katy Trail, as it is popularly called, that will eventually extend nearly 200 miles east to west across central Missouri.

The Busch and Weldon Spring areas are home to a large percentage of the breeding bird species of eastern Missouri, including many forest and streamside birds. These are supplemented by a variety of migrants in spring and fall, and winter brings its own diversity of raptors and passerines. The two areas provide fine birding any day of the year.

Best Sites: Although any part of these areas can be productive, certain favored spots are visited most often by local birders. Refer to area maps available at the headquarters for exact directions.

The following nine areas are located within the *Busch Conservation Area* (Map 9) and are listed in suggested order for a morning visit to cover all habitats.

The *Fallen Oak Nature Trail* **[K-1]**, a loop of 0.7 miles, is located just off the east parking lot at the main entrance and headquarters. The trail passes through a pine woodland where feeders are located in winter, offering good views of such birds as Red-breasted Nuthatch (some winters only), Rufous-sided Towhee, Fox Sparrow, and Purple Finch. The woods has also been used by roosting owls in the winter. Pine Warblers have been noted here in the breeding season.

Hampton Memorial Lake **[K-2]** (often referred to as "Shop Lake"), located just beyond the entrance gate, contains a boardwalk and a viewing blind to aid in observing or photographing waterfowl. Waterfowl consist mainly of Canada Geese, Mallards, and sometimes other puddle ducks. White-fronted Geese have often been sighted at the lake during migration. Bell's Vireo can usually be found each summer along the road that wraps around the north side of the lake. The willows and cottonwoods near the boardwalk harbor Yellow Warbler, Warbling Vireo, and both oriole species.

Bell's Vireo

The *James E. Comfort Forest* **[K-3]**, located on a side road leading north off Road C about one mile west of Hampton Lake, is a pine woods that has in some winters contained Long-eared Owls. This small patch of woods has also provided cover for Screech, Great Horned, Barred, and (rarely) Northern Saw-whet Owls.

Lakes 37 and 38 **[K-4]** at the west side of Busch Conservation Area are separated from each other by a large earth dam. The dam is sometimes used as a "hawk-watch" vantage point during the fall hawk migration. Migrating warblers are often found in the woods that border the east edge of these lakes.

The *Archery Range* **[K-5]** is an area used for bow hunting and archery practice. Birders should park in the parking lot at the top, walk the service road down through the wooded area, and cross the bridge over Kraut Run to the open fields beyond. Because of archers, care should be exercised when going off the road in these woods before crossing the creek. Breeding specialties found on this route include Eastern Wood Pewee, Acadian Flycatcher, Wood Thrush, Yellow-throated and Prothonotary Warblers, Louisiana Waterthrush, and Scarlet Tanager. Lark Sparrow can be found in the open fields. Look overhead for hawks.

Lake 33 **[K-6]** is the largest lake in the area (about 200 acres) and contains water deep enough to attract diving ducks and cormorants during migration and winter. Horned Grebe, Eared Grebe, Osprey, Franklin's and Bonaparte's Gulls, and Forster's Tern have been seen at the lake. At the west (shallow) end of the lake is a modest sized marsh that attracts shorebirds in dry years when the water level is low.

Dardenne Creek **[K-7]** is accessible from the road along the dam on the east end of Lake 33. Proceed to the parking lot and continue on foot along the service road to the creek. Cross the creek, if possible, and continue into the mature woods. Yellow-billed Cuckoo, Barred Owl, Pileated Woodpecker, Acadian Flycatcher, Eastern Phoebe, Blue-gray Gnatcatcher, Yellow-throated and Red-eyed Vireos, Cerulean, Prothonotary, Worm-eating, and Kentucky Warblers, Northern Parula, and

fallen bridge at Dardenne Creek

Louisiana Waterthrush are some of the breeding birds found here.

The *Shorebird Area* **[K-8]**, located east of the Lake 33 dam, is an area managed to attract shorebirds during migration. Some years the management is more successful than others. These two pools have attracted a good variety of shorebirds, commonly including both yellowlegs and the "peep" species, Solitary and Pectoral Sandpipers, and occasionally such rarities as Hudsonian Godwit and Wilson's Phalarope. When the habitat is unsuitable for shorebirds, there are usually some herons, ducks, and swallows. Check adjacent fields for scarce migrant sparrows such as Le Conte's and Sharp-tailed, as well as the commoner Savannah and Swamp, and watch for hawks overhead.

Lakes 24, 34, and 35 **[K-9]** are located beside a loop road off Road C and provide varied habitat with good opportunities for seeing birds. The brushy area on the south side of Lake 24 is good for sparrows and Yellow-rumped Warblers in the winter; it provided cover for a Harris' Sparrow for almost an entire winter. Lake 34 is a fairly deep lake that provides habitat for Common Loons. Lake 35 can be good for waterfowl, Osprey, shorebirds, terns, and swallows; be sure to check the south end, accessed from a small side road.

The following four areas are in the *Weldon Spring Conservation Area* (Map 10).

A trail through *open fields* **[L-1]** is located on the left (south) side of MO-94 about 0.7 miles from the junction of US-40/61. The unnamed trail is an old gravel road that departs from a parking area adjacent to MO-94 and travels through open, uncultivated fields. The weedy fields are good for Loggerhead Shrike, Bell's Vireo, Blue Grosbeak, Dickcissel, and sparrows. In spring, when the fields are wet, Sedge and Marsh Wrens, and even an occasional Sora can be discovered. This site is popular among hunters.

The *Lewis and Clark Hiking Trails* **[L-2]**, which start on the left (south) side of MO-94 about 2.5 miles from the junction of US-40/61, are good for flycatchers, thrushes, vireos, and resident warblers in summer. Walking these trails in winter is a good way to see Pileated and other woodpeckers. At the parking lot just off MO-94, American Woodcock can often be seen and heard in the evening or early morning in spring. The Lewis Trail (formerly, Yellow Trail) makes an 8.2 mile loop; the Clark Trail (Red Trail) is concurrent with the Lewis Trail for much of its length, but takes a shortcut making it only 5.3 miles long. Both trails provide excellent views of the Missouri River and its floodplain from the top of the bluffs above the Katy Trail.

The *Missouri River Public Fishing Access* **[L-3]** is located approximately 2.8 miles further west on MO-94. Turn left at the "Katy Trail" sign. Follow the road down to the trail and across the floodplain to the boat launching ramp at the Missouri River. Here, Bald Eagles can sometimes be found in the winter and Fish Crows in the spring and summer. Horned Larks are seen on the floodplain. The Katy Trail itself, hiked in either direction, provides good land birding if it is not too crowded (watch for bicycles). It is a fine location for a bird walk on a winter morning, when Yellow-rumped Warblers may be found along the bluff.

The *Lost Valley Hiking Biking Trail* **[L-4]** along Little Femme Osage Creek is located another 0.8 miles west on MO-94 beyond the access to the Katy Trail, starting from a parking lot on the right side of MO-94. An old road follows the sycamore-lined creek. This pleasant hike is a reliable way to find Wood Thrush, White-eyed Vireo, Northern Parula, Yellow-throated and Cerulean Warblers, Louisiana Waterthrush, and Yellow-breasted Chat.

Birds: Many of the characteristic species are mentioned under **Best Sites**. In addition to these commoner birds, the areas provide a good place for seeking various species that are scarce or hard to find around St. Louis, such as Willow Flycatcher, and Le Conte's and Sharp-tailed Sparrows. In addition, forty-some years of exploration by local birders have turned up a large number of rarities, bringing the total area list to 280 species. The most unusual finds include Glossy Ibis, Cinnamon Teal, Black Vulture, Yellow Rail, Ruff, Say's Phoebe, Vermilion Flycatcher, Swainson's Warbler, Green-tailed Towhee, Bachman's Sparrow, McCown's Longspur, and Snow Bunting.

Yellow-throated Vireo

General Information: Use of insect repellent is recommended when visiting either area in summer. No camping is permitted within the areas. Busch Conservation Area is open to the public between 6:00 a.m. and 10:00 p.m. from April 1 to September 30 and from 6:00 a.m. to 7:00 p.m. from October 1 to March 31. Weldon Spring Conservation Area is open between 4:00 a.m. and 10:00 p.m. daily. These areas provide outdoor recreation opportunities for hunters, anglers, hikers, dog trainers, horseback riders, archers, and nature study enthusiasts. At certain times, especially in spring and fall, other uses such as hunting and dog trials may seem to preclude a quiet activity like birding, but an astute birder can always locate some places that are off limits to those pursuits (e.g., the shorebird area and some designated hiking trails).

Restrooms are located in the building adjacent to the lodge at the entrance to Busch Conservation Area, and pit toilets are situated near several of the lakes at Busch, but not at Weldon Spring. No fuel, food, or lodging is available within these areas, but all are available along I-70 in St. Charles or further west along US-40/61.

An annual Christmas Bird Count, centered at US-40/61 and MO-94, includes the Busch and Weldon Spring areas as well as Babler State Park, across the river.

CLARENCE CANNON
NATIONAL WILDLIFE REFUGE   [M]
Pike County, Missouri   *(Map 1)*

Attractions: Clarence Cannon refuge, which is part of the Annada Division of the Mark Twain National Wildlife Refuge, contains a number of pools with habitat for shorebirds, marsh birds, and waterfowl.

Directions: Head west on I-70 and take MO-79 for 35 miles north to Annada, Missouri. The sign to Clarence Cannon National Wildlife Refuge is just past the Annada city limits. Turn right, and drive about a mile into the refuge.

Description: Established with money raised from the sale of federal duck stamps, this 3,747 acre refuge lies within the Mississippi River floodplain and is made up of permanent and seasonally flooded impoundments, forests, grasslands, and crop fields. The refuge has an extensive road system allowing birders to view the fields, choosing the best habitat for waterfowl and shorebirds. Water levels are usually kept high to attract waterfowl, but the impoundments are slowly drained in spring, creating mudflats that can attract shorebirds.

Best Sites: Visitors should stop at the office and obtain a refuge map, which shows the main east-west road and the several side roads. Refuge personnel may be able to give directions to the best spots; these vary from year to year and from season to season.

Birds: Located some distance from St. Louis and rather off the beaten path, Clarence Cannon does not get the coverage that it probably deserves. It can be a fine area during waterfowl migration, when any of the species that pass through the St. Louis area can be expected. When water levels are right, there may be shorebirds in the impoundments or along the muddy roadside edges. Among the locally scarce birds known to nest on the refuge are the Least Bittern, Hooded Merganser, Bald Eagle (at this writing, one of the few locations in Missouri), and Marsh Wren. During the nesting season Yellow-throated and Cerulean Warblers may be found in the wooded areas along the levee, and Sedge Wrens and Dickcissels occur in the grassy areas. Other possibilities are Yellow-crowned Night-Heron, Cooper's Hawk, and Loggerhead Shrike in summer, American Pipit and Brewer's Blackbird during migration, and Lapland Longspur in the fields in winter. Exploration of the refuge is encouraged.

General Information: The refuge is open from sunrise to sunset. The visitor center is open from 7:30 a.m. to 4:00 p.m. Monday through Friday. There are no toilet facilities when the visitor center is closed. Restaurants, motels, and service stations are available in nearby Clarksville and Elsberry. The refuge telephone number is (314) 847-2333.

LOCK AND DAM NUMBER 25 AT WINFIELD [N]
Lincoln County, Missouri (Maps 1 & 12)

Attractions: Large concentrations of Bald Eagles and waterfowl are found at the Winfield dam in winter.

Directions: Take I-70 west to MO-79. Drive north on MO-79 for 14 miles to Winfield. Just past the McLean Creek bridge, turn right onto county highway N, as directed by the signs. This road leads to the dam access road on the left and also to riverbottom woods.

Description: The Winfield dam on the Mississippi River has two elevated observation platforms, one next to the lock and dam, the other north of the dam. Just below the dam, a ferry carries cars and passengers to Calhoun County in Illinois (see Map 12).

Best Sites and Birds: In winter, the Winfield Dam affords visitors the opportunity to easily observe Bald Eagles as they roost in trees along the river and feed on fish in the open water below the dam. Rafts of diving ducks, especially Canvasback, and large numbers of Ring-billed and Herring Gulls can also be seen. Occasionally the dam attracts rarer gulls, such as the Glaucous. In winter, watch for hawks and Lapland Longspurs while approaching the dam along the river access road. Check for ducks and gulls on the quiet backwater, just before reaching the dam. In migration, other water birds can also be observed, including Double-crested Cormorant (late summer), White Pelican, Osprey, Franklin's and Bonaparte's Gulls, and various species of terns. Eurasian Tree Sparrows reside in the tall trees and around the visitor's area.

General Information: There are picnic tables and restrooms at the dam.

SHAW ARBORETUM [O]
Franklin County, Missouri (Map 1)

Attractions: Shaw Arboretum offers the best opportunity in the area to see nearly all the bird species characteristic of the Ozarks, including riverbottom birds. It is also a good spot for winter finches because of the numerous coniferous trees.

Directions: Shaw Arboretum is located southwest of St. Louis about 23 miles from the I-44/I-270 junction. Take I-44 west to Gray Summit. Turn left across the overpass, then immediately right; the entrance is just ahead on the left. Maps and trail guides are available at the Visitor's Center (sometimes closed in winter), and maps are also posted near the parking lot and at the Trail House.

Description: Shaw Arboretum is a 2,400-acre nature study area managed by the Missouri Botanical Garden. The property straddles the Meramec River, on the edge of the Ozark plateau, and consists of oak-hickory forest, open fields, glades, edge habitat along the trails and glades, coniferous plantings, river floodplain, and gravel bars.

Best Sites: The Arboretum is a good place to hike and see birds year-round. The various trails provide access to a variety of different habitats.

Pinetum Trail, a one-half mile trail, begins at the Visitor Center at the entrance, passes through conifers, and skirts Pinetum Lake. Red-breasted Nuthatch and (more rarely) crossbills can sometimes be found in the conifers during the winter.

Wolf Run Trail is a one-mile trail through second-growth forest and meadows where Eastern Bluebirds and Blue-winged and Prairie Warblers can often be seen and heard.

Brush Creek Trail, a three-quarter-mile trail, runs through mature forest and a large meadow. It is good for such residents as Blue-gray Gnatcatcher, White-eyed and Yellow-throated Vireos, Northern Parula, Louisiana Waterthrush, and Kentucky Warbler.

Prairie Trail, a one-mile trail, branches off Brush Creek Trail and winds through the high grasses and prairie wildflowers of the Experimental Prairie. Less common species such as Prairie Warbler, Blue Grosbeak, and Henslow's Sparrow have been seen here as well as the more common Yellow-breasted Chat and Common Yellowthroat along the fencerows.

River Trail, a two-mile trail, begins at the end of Brush Creek Trail near the Trail House (look for nesting Eastern Phoebe on the beams above the picnic tables). The trail passes through a variety of natural communities, highlighted by the floodplain forest that contains such breeding species as Acadian Flycatcher and Yellow-throated, Cerulean, and Prothonotary Warblers. From the hillside branch of the trail (named Wildflower Trail), Worm-eating Warblers and Ovenbirds are sometimes heard and seen.

Birds: Aside from the birds mentioned above, breeding non-passerines include Cooper's Hawk, Red-shouldered Hawk, Wild Turkey, Northern Bobwhite, Yellow-billed Cuckoo, Great Horned Owl, Barred Owl, and Pileated Woodpecker. Breeding passerines include five species of flycatchers and at least fourteen species of warblers. Summer Tanager and Orchard Oriole are sometimes found in upland woods and edges.

General Information: The Arboretum is open from 7 a.m. to one-half hour after sunset, seven days a week. Gates are locked promptly. There is a small admission fee for non-members. Facilities are limited, with many roads closed to vehicles. The main loop road is the only road open to vehicular traffic, but it has only a limited number of parking spaces at trailheads. A trail wagon operates during spring and summer, but this is not conducive to good birding. There are restrooms at the Visitor's Center and Trail House and a pay telephone at the Trail House. There is no

Ovenbird

drinking water after the Trail House and nowhere to purchase food on the grounds, but there are restaurants and motels across from the main gate. Between March and November, you may wish to use tick spray and insect repellent. The telephone number is (314) 742-3512.

ST. FRANCOIS STATE PARK   [P]
St. Francois County, Missouri   *(Map 1)*

Attractions: In spring and summer, St. Francois Park is a fine area for seeing breeding birds of old fields and Ozark forest edge, including several species that are less common closer to St. Louis.

Directions: Take I-55 south about 22 miles from I-270 to the US-67 exit, just past the exit for Festus; then follow US-67 south for 19 miles. Watch for road signs to the park entrance on the left. The park is within an hour's drive of St. Louis.

Description: This 2,616-acre park is located in the Ozark border, a natural geographic division south of St. Louis. The upland part of the park is covered with a mixture of oak, hickory, and black gum trees, while sycamore and ash trees line the Big River, running through the bottomland region of the park. The uplands also contain some fields.

Best Sites: Any part of the park may be good for birds, including the campground areas. Usually, local birders plan a trip to St. Francois State Park in late May or early June to see the breeding passerines and raptors. The park is usually active at this time of year with campers, picnickers, and other tourists, but their activities do not generally interfere with birding.

Birds: Birds likely to be seen at St. Francois on a summer trip include Turkey Vulture, Red-tailed and Broad-winged Hawks, Northern Bobwhite, Yellow-billed Cuckoo, Ruby-throated Hummingbird, Eastern Kingbird, Red-eyed Vireo, Blue-winged and Prairie Warblers (in upland areas with cedars and other scrubby growth), Cerulean Warbler and Northern Parula (in tall trees along the river), Summer Tanager, and Orchard Oriole. More difficult to observe because they are scarcer are Mississippi Kite, Cooper's Hawk, Pileated Woodpecker, Bewick's Wren (an early breeder), and Blue Grosbeak.

*Eastern
Kingbird*

General Information: The park is open year round with ample restrooms, campsites, and picnic tables. It is often crowded on weekends. The park telephone number is (314) 358-2173.

HAWN STATE PARK [Q]
Ste. Genevieve County, Missouri (Map 1)

Attractions: Hawn State Park provides the only consistent breeding ground in the St. Louis area for the Pine Warbler. It's also one of the best places in the area to combine a long hike with a serious birding trip.

Directions: From St. Louis, drive south on I-55 from I-270 for 42 miles to county highway O. Turn right (west) on county highway O to MO-32, approximately 12 miles. Turn right onto MO-32 and continue to MO-144. Turn left onto MO-144 and drive to the park headquarters. The drive takes at least one hour from the junction of I-270 and I-55 to the park entrance.

Description: Hawn State Park (3,271-acres) is in an unusual area of the state where exposures of sandstone bedrock create a landscape of rounded knobs, canyon-rimmed valleys, and vertical cliffs above clear, sandy-bottomed streams. Birders with an interest in botany will notice plants that are normally found further north, including rattlesnake orchid and ground pine. Hikers and backpackers on the 10-mile Whispering Pine Trail can explore knobs, ridges, glades, and the River aux Vases, which runs through the south part of the park. The mile-long Pickle Creek Trail, near the campground and picnic area, traverses sandstone bluffs, granite shut-ins, and Pickle Creek, which will remind visitors of a cascading mountain stream.

Best Sites and Birds: Pine Warblers are most easily found in the conifers around the headquarters. Chipping Sparrows, which have a song that can be confused with the Pine Warbler's song, also occur in the pines. Broad-winged Hawks and Wild Turkeys nest in the area. Songbirds that favor extensive tracts of undivided forest, such as Wood Thrush and Scarlet Tanager, also nest in the park. Worm-eating Warblers can be found on the hillsides, and Prairie Warblers can be found in park glades and by driving the roads, such as Hawn Park Road to the west of the park. Ozark streamside birds such as Acadian Flycatcher, Eastern Phoebe, and Louisiana Waterthrush are common. A chorus of Whip-Poor-Wills can be heard by overnight campers in late spring or early summer. As one approaches the park after leaving the interstate, watch the wires and fences for Eastern Bluebird, Loggerhead Shrike, Blue Grosbeak, Indigo Bunting, Dickcissel, Lark Sparrow, and Grasshopper Sparrow.

General Information: Park brochures are available at the headquarters. Campsites are available on a first-come, first-served basis. Water is turned off from the first of November until the first of April. Restrooms are available at the campsites and pit toilets at the picnic areas. The park is busy on weekends. The park telephone number is (314) 883-3603.

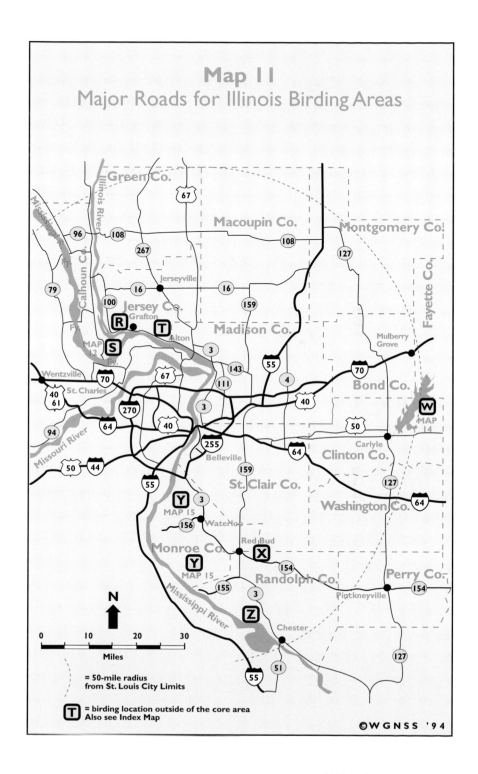

Map 11
Major Roads for Illinois Birding Areas

Green Co.

Macoupin Co.

Montgomery Co.

Fayette Co.

67

96 108

267

79

16 Jerseyville 16

159

100 Jersey Co.

R Grafton

T

S Alton

Madison Co.

Mulberry Grove

3

143 55

Wentzville 70

67 111 4 70 Bond Co.

40 61 St. Charles

270 3

40 W MAP 14

94 64 40

Missouri River

50 44

255 Belleville

64 Clinton Co.

Carlyle

50

50 44

50

127

159

55 55

Y 3

MAP 15

156 Waterloo

St. Clair Co.

Washington Co. 64

Monroe Co.

Y

MAP 15

Red Bud

X 154

Perry Co.

155 3 Randolph Co.

Pinckneyville

154

Mississippi River

Z

Chester

127

N

0   10   20   30

Miles

51

55

= 50-mile radius
from St. Louis City Limits

T = birding location outside of the core area
Also see Index Map

©WGNSS '94

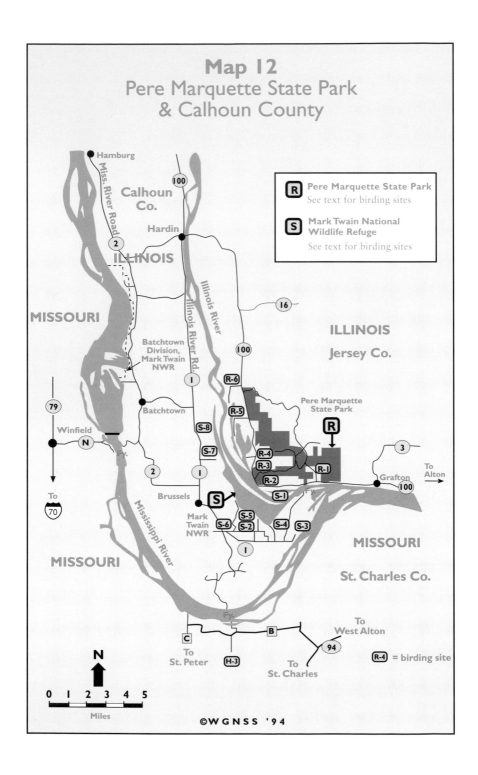

Map 12
Pere Marquette State Park
& Calhoun County

Hamburg

Miss. River Road

Calhoun Co.

100

Hardin

2

ILLINOIS

MISSOURI

R Pere Marquette State Park
See text for birding sites

S Mark Twain National Wildlife Refuge
See text for birding sites

16

Illinois River

Illinois River Rd.

100

Batchtown Division, Mark Twain NWR

I

R-6

R-5

Batchtown

S-8

79

S-7

ILLINOIS
Jersey Co.

Pere Marquette State Park

R

3

Winfield

N

Fy.

2

I

R-4

R-3

R-1

To Alton

Grafton

100

R-2

Brussels

To
70

S

S-1

Fy.

Mississippi River

Mark Twain NWR

S-6

S-5
S-2

S-4

S-3

I

MISSOURI

St. Charles Co.

MISSOURI

Fy.

To West Alton

C

B

94

To St. Peter

H-3

To St. Charles

R-4 = birding site

N

0 1 2 3 4 5
Miles

©WGNSS '94

PERE MARQUETTE STATE PARK   [R]
Jersey County, Illinois   *(Maps 12 & 11)*

Attractions: Pere Marquette State Park offers good birding for land birds in all seasons, plus fine views of the Illinois River valley. A trip here can be combined with birding in the nearby **Mark Twain National Wildlife Refuge [S]**.

Directions: The park entrance is located on IL-100 (Great River Road) west of Alton and Grafton. Birding can start at the main entrance near the lodge on IL-100 (6.5 miles west of Grafton) or from Graham Hollow Road off IL-100 (2.6 miles west of Grafton).

Description: Pere Marquette is the largest state park in Illinois, with a total area of 8,000 acres. It is hilly, being situated on limestone bluffs bordering the Illinois River. Much of the area is covered with second-growth timber, most of which is mature forest. Stands of coniferous trees are scattered throughout the park. In a few places, the loess hills are open and covered with native grasses. The park contains over 15 miles of foot trails and bridle paths.

Best Sites: A good variety of land birds can be found along **Graham Hollow Road [R-1]**, which winds along a wooded creek, open fields, and second-growth hillsides. Turn north (right) off IL-100 about 2.6 miles past Grafton on Graham Hollow Road. A good stop is where the road forks, about 1.3 miles from IL-100. A walk on either side of the road can be productive, especially during migration. Over 50 species of birds are known to nest in the area. Follow the left fork off Graham Hollow Road to the top of the hill where another left turn leads to a series of overlook points, which provide good views of the Illinois River and Swan Lake. Land birds and occasionally hawks can be seen at these stops. Walking the nearby trails and bridle paths can also be fruitful.

The overlook road eventually descends the bluff to **Pere Marquette Lodge [R-2]** at the main entrance. At the bottom of the hill, turn left at the stop sign and into the lodge parking lot. The wooded areas around the lodge and cabins and above the campgrounds provide good birding any time of the year.

Across IL-100 from the park entrance, pull into the parking lot. Here you can view **Stump Lake [R-3]**, a boat harbor, and the Illinois River. This site provides good birding for water-loving birds in all seasons. The woods around Stump Lake (state managed) attract warblers and other land birds.

Proceed west and north on IL-100 about 2.1 miles past the main park entrance and turn left onto **Dabbs Road [R-4]** (gravel). Continue past the pumping station to the parking lot. A levee extends from the edge of the parking lot across upper Stump Lake. If time permits, two additional roads farther north on IL-100 may be productive, **Long Lake Road [R-5]** and **Glades Road [R-6]**.

the lodge

Birds: The park is a good place to find migrating warblers in spring. Breeding birds along Graham Hollow Road include several species of flycatchers, White-eyed Vireo, Blue-winged and Kentucky Warblers, Northern Parula, Ovenbird, Summer and Scarlet Tanagers, Northern Oriole, and American Goldfinch. Turkey Vultures are ever-present in summer. Birding the trails atop the bluffs can produce Worm-eating Warbler, vireos, tanagers, and cuckoos. In the bottomland forest surrounding Stump Lake, Pileated Woodpecker, Acadian Flycatcher, Warbling Vireo, and Prothonotary Warbler can usually be found. Herons, egrets, and occasionally Yellow-crowned Night-Herons as well as waterfowl (except during the hunting season) are found at Stump Lake. From the overlooks in September and October, American White Pelicans may sometimes be spotted on Swan Lake, although a good look requires a spotting scope. Migrant and wintering gulls can be found at the boat harbor. Wintering Bald Eagles are commonly found in the trees along the Illinois River.

General Information: The park is open from 8:00 a.m. to 9:00 p.m. Restrooms are available at the lodge, and pit toilets are located elsewhere in the park. Hunting is permitted within certain areas of the park during statewide seasons that vary from year to year; at these times much of the park is off limits to birders. The lodge has dining facilities and 72 rooms, but reservations are required. Cabins are also available and camping is permitted in the campground. The telephone number is (618) 786-2331.

A Christmas Bird Count, centered at Meppen in Calhoun County, is held each year that covers the park, the Mark Twain refuge, and surrounding areas of Jersey and Calhoun Counties.

MARK TWAIN NATIONAL WILDLIFE REFUGE   [S]

Jersey and Calhoun Counties, Illinois   *(Maps 12 & 11)*

Attractions: Areas of open water on the Mark Twain Refuge attract large numbers of waterfowl and other water-loving birds. The adjacent woodlands and fields provide good birding for land birds and raptors.

Directions: To reach Gilbert Lake, take IL-100 west from Grafton to 0.2 miles past the Brussels Ferry landing. The entrance is on the left side of the road. To reach Swan Lake, take the Brussels Ferry (free) across the Illinois River. Continue 3.6 miles on Illinois River Road to a gravel road on the right; follow signs to the refuge headquarters.

Description: Several divisions of the refuge lie along a 250-mile stretch of the Mississippi River from southern Iowa south to Calhoun County, Illinois. Together, these divisions constitute the only National Wildlife Refuge in our area (see also location **[M]**). Most of the refuge consists of sloughs and oxbows adjacent to the river and the bordering bottomland woods; at many points land portions of the refuge are less than a quarter-mile wide. We are concerned here with two divisions of the Brussels District of the refuge, the Gilbert Lake Division in Jersey County and the Swan Lake portion of the Calhoun Division in Calhoun County. Both divisions are managed to provide food, shelter, and habitat for wildlife. Water levels are manipulated to encourage vegetation for birds. Gilbert Lake contains about 225 acres of water and has a three-mile road (no vehicles) that begins at IL-100 and terminates at the Pere Marquette State Park marina complex. The road follows the Illinois River through bottomland forests and farm fields. Swan Lake, an oxbow of the Illinois River that is connected to the river at the lower end, contains about 3,000 acres of water and has extensive bottomland forests along the shore.

Best Sites: *Gilbert Lake* **[S-1]** (Jersey County) is good in spring and fall for waterfowl and shorebirds. The bottomland forests are a good place to seek migrant and resident land birds. Birders can walk the access road as far as desired and then return by the same route, or hike all the way to the boat ramp at Pere Marquette State Park (3 miles).

To reach *Calhoun County* and *Swan Lake*, cross the Illinois River on the Brussels Ferry and continue for about three miles along Illinois River Road. In winter, watch for geese in the fields on the right side. Make a left turn, and follow the sign to the *Royal Landing* **[S-3]**, which provides access to the Mississippi River. A foot trail through the adjacent woods leads toward the junction of the Illinois and Mississippi Rivers. The bottomland forest is home to several pairs of Pileated Woodpeckers.

Return to Illinois River Road, continue 0.6 miles, and turn right on the gravel road that leads to a *pump station* **[S-4]**. Watching for water birds along the road, drive 0.7 miles to a levee on the left that extends into a moist soil unit. Bird the levee for shorebirds, rails, and sparrows. Continue on the road to the pump and park at the gate. Ahead is Swan Lake, which can be viewed by walking a short distance along a drainage ditch to a lookout point on the shore. Some distance off to the right, toward the junction of Swan Lake and the Illinois River channel, there is often a large aggregation of ducks and gulls. From the pump, continue walking east on the road toward the equipment (storage) shed. Check the pool to the right of and behind the shed for waterfowl and herons. From the rear of the shed, continue birding along the road through the woods to just past a culvert. Walk left to the edge of the lake; this spot provides an excellent view toward the Illinois River. (The shed was damaged during the 1993 floods and may be removed in the future).

Return to Illinois River Road and continue 1.2 miles west. Turn right and follow the signs to the *refuge headquarters* **[S-2]**. A visit to the headquarters area is recommended, even on weekends when the office is not open. The nearby pond and prairie grasses can be productive and the deck of the headquarters building provides a good vantage point from which to scan for raptors. Continue on the dirt road downhill toward Swan Lake, and park at the barrier (or simply walk down from the office). From the barrier, walk on the road through the mature bottomland woods to the lakeshore. Scan the lake for waterfowl, then turn around and walk back toward the gate. After about a hundred feet, turn right, enter the woods, and walk parallel to the lakeshore. Shortly you will come to a small creek. Follow the creek to the lake. The delta of the creek forms a point that local birders call the *"volcano"* **[S-5]**; it is good in fall for sparrows and shorebirds or at any time as a place to scan the lake for waterfowl. The last part of the walk, near the lake edge, may be quite muddy and weedy.

After leaving the refuge office, return to the first crossroad (Deer Plain Road), turn right, and go one mile. Turn right on the first unmarked road, called *Sand Ridge Road* **[S-6]**. The rough gravel road looks forbidding, as it is marked with threatening signs, but be assured that it is a public road and provides access to the northern end of Swan Lake. Follow the road (first gravel, then packed sand) for 2.5 miles. Just beyond a little bridge, the road turns left, parallel to the lake shore; shortly, there is an unmarked dirt track to the right, leading to an opening in the trees and a vantage point on the lake shore. Park there. Stay on the lake side of the road, for the opposite side is private property.

From Sand Ridge, return to Deer Plain Road, turn right, and continue west until the road ends at Illinois River Road; turn right, and proceed on Illinois River Road for 4.6 miles. (Alternatively, from the refuge headquarters, return to Illinois River Road, turn right, and drive directly about 8 miles.) Look for a gravel road on the right marked *"Bim's Road"* *(850 N)* **[S-7]**. Drive the road past farms and cottages to the access road on upper Swan Lake. Bird here for waterfowl, shorebirds, and gulls.

Continue north 4.5 miles past Bim's Road. Just past a farm house, turn right at a sign marked "Hadley Landing" *(1300N)*. Drive the road to a sign marked *"Fuller Lake"* **[S-8]**. Turn right, and drive through a bottomland woods. This woods is good birding year round. The water in Fuller Lake is normally drawn down in August, when it can be good for shorebirds.

If time permits, the farmland and apple orchards of southern Calhoun Co. (south of Brussels) are hilly and scenic. It is a fine region to explore for birds from fall through spring because it is interspersed with woods and vegetated fencerows (look for Eurasian Tree Sparrows) and is not so extensively cultivated as the prairie regions to the east. One can return to St. Charles Co. via the Golden Eagle Ferry (toll), except in winter.

Birds: The refuge and the farmland around it constitute one of the best birding sites in the St. Louis area. Waterfowl, seen mainly on Gilbert and Swan Lakes, are a primary attraction, although the flocks move around and may sometimes be hard to see from the vantage points described above (a spotting scope is usually necessary). Twenty species of ducks are regular, but the big attraction in winter is the concentration of Snow Geese, often numbering ten thousand or more. This is the northernmost wintering flock of Snow Geese in the Mississippi River valley. The birds may be found feeding in the refuge fields, sometimes right by the highway. Ross's Geese have been found among the Snows by those with the patience to check carefully. Several thousand Canada Geese may also be present, joined in migration by White-fronted Geese. Swan Lake also attracts many other water birds such as loons, grebes, cormorants, terns, and gulls (Bonaparte's and Franklin's Gulls are regular migrants among the abundant Ring-billed Gulls). American White Pelicans, usually found here each fall, may be visible from the Sand Ridge Road vantage point. In summer and fall, the numbers of herons and egrets lining the lake shore can be spectacular. Look for Yellow-crowned Night-Herons on the pump station/equipment shed road.

The refuge area is one of the best places to look for raptors. In winter, Bald Eagles are the most evident raptor, although Northern Harriers,

American Kestrels, and Red-tailed Hawks (including an occasional Harlan's) are also common. Rough-legged Hawks and accipiters are uncommon. Migration brings many Ospreys and Broad-winged Hawks, as well as a few Peregrine Falcons. Shorebird populations depend on water levels and the extent of muddy edge around the lakes or flooding in the fields. Grassy areas (e.g., near the refuge office) have resident Eastern Meadowlark, Bobwhite, and Ring-necked Pheasant, plus a variety of sparrows in season. Regularly occurring sparrows include American Tree, Song, Swamp, Savannah, and sometimes LeConte's. Open croplands nearby accommodate Horned Larks and sometimes Lapland Longspurs in winter. Breeding birds in the bottomland forests include Barred Owl, all of the resident woodpeckers, Eastern Wood-Pewee, Acadian Flycatcher, Black-capped Chickadee, Warbling Vireo, American Redstart, and Prothonotary Warbler. Eurasian Tree Sparrows are generally easy to find at the refuge office, or along the Illinois River by the ferry landing. Birders have accumulated a long list of "good finds" on the refuge, some of which have proved to be fairly regular over the years (e.g., Tundra Swan). Whatever the season, the birder can hope for something rare, perhaps a Sabine's Gull on Swan Lake, a Prairie Falcon over the farmland, an American Avocet in a flooded field, or a Sharp-tailed Sparrow along the marshy edge.

General Information: The refuge office and visitor center is open 7:30 a.m. to 4:00 p.m., Monday through Friday. The refuge is closed annually during the hunting season, October 15 to December 15. There are other access roads to Swan Lake, but these involve trespassing across private property. Birders should respect the rights of landowners and ask permission before entry. Flooding of the area can occur any time of the year but is most likely in the spring. High water may flood only certain fields, or it may completely cover the whole area. The telephone number of the refuge headquarters is (618) 883-2524.

THE GREAT RIVER ROAD [T]
Madison and Jersey Counties, Illinois (Map 6)

Attractions: A trip along the Great River Road in winter or during migration is a good way to see eagles, gulls, and ducks. Some of the river access points may offer habitat for shorebirds.

Directions: All of the areas described here are points of access to the Mississippi River that occur in Illinois. To reach these areas from St.

Louis, the two most convenient bridges across the Mississippi River are the I-270 bridge and the Clark bridge (US-67) at Alton. The McKinley bridge ($0.50 toll) offers quick access to Lock No. 27 in Granite City, but the road bed is in poor condition at this writing.

The tour described here takes the birder downstream from Grafton to Lock No. 27. (Note that for all but the last few miles of this route, the Mississippi River flows mainly west to east, not north to south.) The route, of course, can be reversed or started at any of the three bridges mentioned above. Local birders often visit *Horseshoe Lake* **[U]** first and then follow the Great River Road from Brooklyn north to Alton. Birders on US-67/IL-143 who wish to continue from Alton to Grafton and the *Mark Twain National Wildlife Refuge* **[S]** should turn left onto IL-100 at the flour mills in Alton (this can lead to a long day of birding). Birders starting the trip at the Clark bridge will want to visit the *Riverlands Environmental Demonstration Area* **[G]**.

Description: The Mississippi River offers good opportunities to view water birds, especially during migration, and the Great River Road offers several salient points for observing them. From Brooklyn north to Alton, the road runs adjacent to the Mississippi River, but the river itself is not always visible from the road or accessible, except at the points listed. However, from Alton to Grafton, a distance of twenty miles, the Mississippi River is in full view from the Great River Road. With the river on one side and tall bluffs on the other, this route is one of the most scenic in the St. Louis area and can be a pleasant drive in any season, even if birds are scarce. The Great River Road is a four-lane divided highway most of its length, and parking along the road is usually adequate, with frequent turn-off points.

Best Sites: Located at the confluence of the Mississippi and Illinois Rivers, the small town of *Grafton* **[T-1]** provides good restaurants and good views of the Illinois River at the boat ramp. See separate entries for *Pere Marquette State Park* **[R]** and the *Mark Twain National Wildlife Refuge* **[S]**, both just west of Grafton.

A pulloff at *Chautauqua* **[T-2]**, located two miles east of Grafton, offers a good spot to view the Mississippi River. *Elsah* **[T-3]**, located five miles east of Grafton, is a quaint, historical village that has produced winter finches, including Evening Grosbeaks, at local feeders. At Clifton Terrace, 5.5 miles east of Elsah, park on the side of the road to view wintering and migrant ducks and gulls. Check the bluffs along the river all the way to Alton for Bald Eagles, Turkey Vultures, hawks, and falcons.

The *Alton Barge Terminal* **[T-4]** is on a river access road located 0.9 miles east of the Clark bridge on IL-143 (watch for the sign to the entrance on the right). Once you have turned right and gone through the levee floodgate, the road splits to the left and right, offering a good view of the Mississippi River. On the north side of IL-143, immediately across from the Alton Barge Terminal, is a wide, paved road that dead-ends after a quarter mile. A creek and a marsh on both sides of the road frequently offer good water bird habitat. Near the dead end, a small road can be taken to the right. This road, mostly unpaved, can be driven for some distance, but it is not well known or birded, although a Purple Gallinule and Western Kingbird have been sighted here.

The *Melvin Price Dam* **[T-5]** is located 2 miles east of the Clark bridge on the south side of the Great River Road opposite the power plant. The public viewing area is limited now, but in the next few years, after the construction has been completed, the view of the river below the dam should be better.

To view the mudflats of the *Alton power plant* **[T-6]**, return to the Great River Road (IL-143) and continue east. The power plant is 1.3 miles east of the barge terminal; however, the mudflats cannot be viewed from the eastbound lane. Therefore, one must pass the power plant and make a U-turn to get into the westbound lane to view the pond and mudflats after pulling off the road onto the paved shoulder. Sometimes the mudflats offer shorebird habitat, but they are an especially good spot for resting gulls. Return to the eastbound lane at the stoplight at the dam entrance.

From the dam to Granite City, the Great River Road runs parallel to the Mississippi River, but viewing the river is possible only at the access points listed below. Continue southeast on IL-143 and turn right (south) on IL-3.

At Hartford, turn right onto *Hawthorne Street* **[T-7]** at the stoplight and park on the right shoulder. Located 4 miles from the Price Dam, this stop, with ponds on both sides, is best during shorebird migration; the water level is sometimes low enough to provide extensive muddy edge and good shorebird variety. Continue a short distance to the river to scan for cormorants, ducks, eagles, gulls, or terns, depending on the season.

The *Lewis and Clark Historic Site* **[T-8]**, located 2 miles south of Hartford, lies very close to the embarkation point of the Lewis and Clark Expedition of 1804. The memorial offers the best view of the confluence of the Mississippi and Missouri Rivers. Prothonotary Warblers can be found here.

To reach the *Chain of Rocks* **[T-9]** access point, return to IL-3 and continue south 3.3 miles. Just past the junction of the Great River Road

(IL-3) and I-270, turn right at the first stoplight onto Chain of Rocks Road. Shortly, you will cross a bridge over the Chain of Rocks Canal. (Alternatively, the same point can be reached by following the levee road along the Chain of Rocks Canal from just south of the Lewis and Clark Historic Site to the canal bridge.) Continue west on Chain of Rocks Road a distance of approximately 2 miles from IL-3 to the abandoned bridge (closed to traffic) across the Mississippi River at Chain of Rocks. At the end of the pavement, turn left, and continue on the gravel road to the river's edge. There is ample parking at this access, even when many fishermen are using the area. The site provides an excellent view (best before noon on a sunny day) of what appears to be a natural rapids, but is actually Dam No. 27, the last dam on the Mississippi River. This is the only shallow and undredged section of the river in the area because barge traffic uses the Chain of Rocks Canal. The rapids and dam attract gulls.

South of the parking lot is the largest expanse of sandy beach in the St. Louis area, but only when water levels are normal or low. In times of high water the parking lot is unreachable. The shoreline extends for a long distance and offers good habitat for plovers and other shorebirds. Search the beach for Buff-breasted Sandpiper, Ruddy Turnstone, and Sanderling (a spotting scope is recommended). Local birders often walk downstream to the first rock dike. This long trek through loose sand in August and September can be arduous, particularly if you are carrying a spotting scope. If the river is high, one can reach the dike through the woods on the riverbank, but this can be a hiking adventure. In winter the area is good for Bald Eagles and gulls.

To reach *Lock No. 27* **[T-10]**, which is at the south end of the Chain of Rocks Canal, return to the Great River Road. Turn right, and go south for five miles to the well marked entrance, which is on the right. This spot is best in mid-winter, mainly for gulls and waterfowl. There is ample parking, and on weekdays during working hours public restrooms are open.

Birds: Along the Mississippi River birders can expect to see any of a number of species of "water birds," with gulls and ducks being most prominent. There are also plenty of passerines that use the bottomland woods for migration and nesting. In late summer and early fall, thousands of swallows feed over the river. Mudflats and sandflats will have shorebirds in season, but such flats are limited in number and unpredictable in occurrence. Raptors may be seen at any point, but especially over the bluffs from Alton to Grafton. In particular, the Bald Eagle is a characteristic winter bird of the riverbanks, visible by the dozens at some of the lookout points.

General Information: The Lewis and Clark Historic Site and Chain of Rocks area are difficult to reach in wet weather as the access roads are muddy. Restaurants and service stations can be found in Alton and at the intersection of I-270 and Chain of Rocks Road with IL-3.

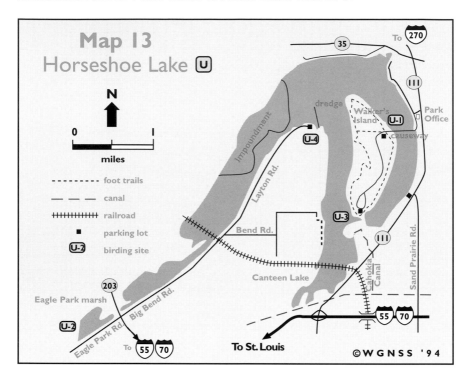

HORSESHOE LAKE [U]
Madison County, Illinois *(Maps 13, 3, & 6)*

Attractions: Horseshoe Lake is a good place to find herons, ducks, gulls, terns, and other birds that are attracted to water. It is one of the most easily accessible birding locations from downtown St. Louis.

Directions: Take I-55/I-70 east from downtown. The lake lies just north of I-55/I-70, 3-4 freeway miles east of the Mississippi River, and can be accessed from the east or the west side.

For the west side (which comes first, as you approach from St. Louis), take IL-203 north past an auto racetrack to the second stoplight at Big Bend Road. Here, turn left a short distance to Eagle Park marsh (see below) or right for Horseshoe Lake proper. After your right turn, Big Bend Road follows the lake margin and crosses a railroad track. The road then forks; Big Bend Road veers to the right through open fields, while Layton Road continues straight ahead along the lake edge until you reach Horseshoe Lake State Park. At the farthest parking area, there is a dredging barge where birds are often attracted. ("Big Bend Road" is often called "Bend Road" by local birders, and is so-labeled at the intersection of Layton Road. However, at IL-203 and on most maps it is "Big Bend Road.")

For the east side of the lake, return to I-55/I-70, continue east to the next exit at IL-111, and go north 3.0 miles, past Canteen Lake, to the entrance of the State Park. This same point can also be reached from northern St. Louis by heading east on I-270, exiting at IL-111, and going south 4.5 miles. Follow the main park road across the causeway to Walker's Island (see below).

Description: Horseshoe Lake is a large, natural oxbow lake. Some water remains open throughout the winter because of warm-water seepage from cooling ponds of the adjacent steel mill. While the lake is the feature of primary interest here, the surrounding portions of *Horseshoe Lake State Park* **[U-1]** (a mixture of cultivated fields, brushy habitats, sloughs, and small woodland tracts) can be of interest to birders as well. Just west of the lake, *Eagle Park marsh* **[U-2]** provides habitat and a breeding area for some species that are not easily found elsewhere in the area. Other small marsh areas lie north and east of the lake (mostly along IL-111).

Best Sites and Birds: Horseshoe Lake is perhaps best known to birders for its herons and egrets. All species regularly occurring in the area have been seen here; Snowy Egrets and Little Blue Herons can be found in large numbers, particularly in July and August. Especially noteworthy are the Black-crowned Night-Herons, of which there is a nearby nesting colony; a few Yellow-crowned Night-Herons occur, also. Birds are best observed from the *causeway* **[U-1]** to Walker's Island, the south end of *Walker's Island* **[U-3]**, or near the sand dredge at the end of *Layton Road* **[U-4]**.

Waterfowl can be seen in large numbers all over the lake in spring. In fall, hunting forces the birds to use the west arm of the lake, between the railroad tracks and the east end of Layton Road. Loons, grebes, and cormorants are especially fond of the deep-water area near the sand dredge, while gulls and a few shorebirds are often present on the sandy spit beyond the dredge pipe. In August and September, the water south of the causeway is sometimes lowered, providing shorebird habitat. In winter, the lake is good place to see gulls. Such rarities as Little, Sabine's, Common Black-headed, Glaucous, and Great and Lesser Black-backed

Gulls have been found. In migration, Bonaparte's and Franklin's Gulls and all five species of terns have occurred.

In drought years, much of the lake can dry up, creating extensive shorebird habitat. In any year, however, there is usually some mudflat on a peninsula visible from the south end of Walker's Island. The peninsula is the result of silt carried into the lake by the Cahokia Canal from the surrounding agricultural lands and presents a threat to the continued viability of the lake.

the dredge, Horseshoe Lake

The campground area and a four-mile nature trail on Walker's Island and the brushy areas at the ends of Layton and Big Bend Roads provide places to seek land birds, including Northern Bobwhite. Le Conte's, Vesper, and Savannah Sparrows are regular migrants, while Sharp-tailed, Harris's, and Henslow's Sparrows are sometimes encountered. Nesting passerines include Willow Flycatcher, Bell's Vireo, and Blue Grosbeak. Eurasian Tree Sparrows can be found on Walker's Island or along Layton Road. Canteen Lake, located on the west side of IL-111 just south of the railroad track, sometimes attracts gulls and ducks.

Eagle Park marsh **[U-2]**, just west of IL-203 on Eagle Park Road (continuous with Big Bend Road), is an interesting stop whenever there is open water (except during hunting season). American Coots nest here annually, as well as small numbers of Pied-billed Grebe and Common Moorhen. Other nesting birds have included Ruddy Duck and Yellow-headed Blackbird (both unexpected and somewhat out of range), and Least Bittern (scarce, but expected). Rails, shorebirds, and most species of waterfowl can be seen during migration, depending on the water level.

General Information: During the fall hunting season, access to the causeway and Walker's Island is prohibited. The land bordering the lake along Big Bend Road is private from IL-203 to the railroad tracks. Pit toilets are located in all park areas. Camping is available on a seasonal basis on Walker's Island; check at headquarters.

FRANK HOLTEN STATE PARK [V]
St. Clair County, Illinois *(Map 3)*

Attractions: Holten State Park is easily reached from downtown St. Louis and is a good place to see herons, egrets, and other water birds.

Directions: Take I-64 east, past East St. Louis to Exit 6. Turn right, and go south on IL-111, which ends at Lake Drive after about 1.5 miles. Turn right on Lake Drive (the northwest boundary of the park), and you will find yourself at the park entrance.

Description: Holten State Park consists of 1,088 acres containing three small lakes with grassy and wooded margins. Two of these are connected and located on the west side of I-255 (which bisects the park but does not provide any access to it). The other is on the east side of I-255 and is accessed by a park road across an overpass. The park was formerly more popular as a birding area before Horseshoe Lake became available as a state park. Horseshoe Lake is now considered superior for birding and Holten State Park has been undeservedly neglected.

Best Sites: The lakes are all viewable from Lake Drive, which runs along the northeast side of the lakes. The road has many pulloffs and parking areas.

Yellow-crowned Night-Heron

Birds: In spite of the inroads of civilization, this park remains one of the best areas to find Yellow-crowned Night-Herons, Cattle Egrets, and Little Blue Herons. Terns occur during migration, and many early gull records also came from the park, including the first area Little Gull. Cliff Swallows have nested under the lake bridge on the west side.

General Information: The park has no provisions for camping. It is used extensively for fishing (boats and shoreline), jogging and picnicking.

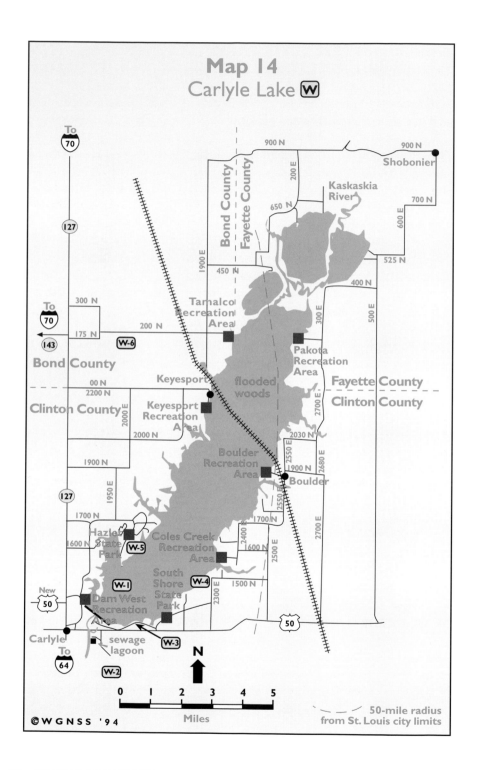

Map 14
Carlyle Lake Ⓦ

To
70

127

Bond County

Fayette County

900 N   900 N
Shobonier

200 E

Kaskaskia
River   700 N

650 N   600 E

525 N

1900 E

450 N   400 N

To
70   300 N

300 E   500 E

143   175 N   200 N   W-6

Tamalco
Recreation
Area

Bond County

Pakota
Recreation
Area

Keyesport   Fayette County

2200 N   flooded
00 N   woods   Clinton County

2000 E

Clinton County   Keyesport
Recreation
Area   2700 E

2000 N

2030 N

1900 N   Boulder
Recreation
Area

2550 E
2550 N

1950 E

2680 E
1900 E

Boulder

127   2550 N

1700 N   1700 N   2700 E

Hazlet
State
Park   Coles Creek
Recreation
Area

1600 N   W-5   2400 E   1600 N   2500 E

New
50   W-1   South
Shore
State
Park   W-4   1500 N   50

Dam West
Recreation
Area

Carlyle

To
64   sewage
lagoon   W-3

W-2   N

0   1   2   3   4   5

©WGNSS '94   Miles

50-mile radius
from St. Louis city limits

CARLYLE LAKE [W]

Clinton and Bond Counties, Illinois (Maps 14 & 11)

Attractions: The largest lake in our area, Carlyle Lake has produced numerous rare birds, mostly in fall.

Directions: Carlyle Lake is approximately 50 miles east of downtown St. Louis (a 75-minute drive by car). Enter Illinois on I-55/I-64/I-70. After a mile, turn east onto I-64, continue to exit 19, and exit north on US-50/IL-158. Within 0.5 miles turn right on US-50 and continue through Lebanon about 24 miles to IL-127 at Carlyle. Turn left, and follow IL-127 a short distance to the next right turn. This road is marked "Dam West Recreation Area." Follow the road to the lake. For specific directions to various birding areas, see **Best Sites** below.

On the way to Carlyle Lake local birders often make a quick side trip to the *O'Fallon sewage lagoon*, which attracts migrating and wintering ducks. After exiting I-64 onto US-50, proceed 1.5 miles and turn left on Reider Road. Proceed 1 mile and park on the right in front of a gate. From this vantage point the entire lagoon can be viewed with a spotting scope without violating the "No Trespassing" signs.

Description: Carlyle Lake was formed by the U. S. Army Corps of Engineers in 1966 with a dam across the Kaskaskia River. The lake is 26,000 acres in size (in summer) with 11,000 acres of public land surrounding it. It is generally rectangular in shape, 2 to 3 miles wide and 15 miles long, with approximately 83 miles of shoreline. The southern portion of the lake is a seasonal waterfowl refuge area, while the northern part is a wildlife management area used for hunting.

Best Sites: To get to *Dam West Recreation Area* **[W-1]** after entering the area as described above, follow the road past the marina and boat ramp to the picnic area on the left. The sand beach at the lake's edge here may have some resting gulls or a few shorebirds. Next, proceed beyond the visitor center and administration building and turn left onto a road that runs below the dam, past a "nature trail" area, and on to a parking lot beside the spillway. Take the steps up to the viewing area atop the dam, which provides an excellent view of the lake, with water birds often visible by the hundreds, near and far. Other birds that might be seen from the dam include raptors aloft or American Pipits and Savannah Sparrows on the dam itself.

To reach the *Carlyle sewage lagoons* **[W-2]**, return to IL-127 and go south through Carlyle to the stoplight. Turn left (east) and follow US-50 past the Spillway Recreation Area (on left) and Fish Hatchery (on right). Just past the Fish Hatchery, turn right, and drive under the narrow railroad bridge. Just past the bridge, there is a gravel road to the right. Park and walk down the road past the locked gate to the lagoons, where gulls and waterfowl may be seen at close range as they rest. The adjacent woods and weedy railroad right-of-way harbor a variety of passerines.

The *saddle dam road* **[W-3]** can be reached by returning to US-50 and turning right (east). Drive about one mile (just over the hill), and turn left at a sign marked "Dam East Recreation Area." After several hundred feet, turn right, and follow the road along the top of the saddle dam. Good waterfowl birding can be found along both sides of the road. Follow the road to the *Green Meadows* boat launch area on the left, which provides another good view of the lake.

Next, follow the saddle dam road to the east end and turn left into *South Shore State Park* **[W-4]**. Hickory Hollow and Deer Run picnic areas are good points from which to scan the lake for loons, grebes, gulls, and waterfowl.

Eldon Hazlet State Park **[W-5]** is on the west side of the lake. Return to IL-127, and go north about 4 miles from Carlyle to the marked road *(1700 N)* leading east to the park. One of the best views of the lake within the park is at the Peppenhorst small boat ramp.

Tamalco Road **[W-6]** is also on the west side of the lake. Take IL-127 about ten miles north to Tamalco Road *(175N)*, turn right, and drive east. Before coming to the first right angle bend in the road after about 0.5 miles, there is good habitat for longspurs in winter. Continuing on this road takes one to the Tamalco Recreation Area boat ramp. From the parking lot, as one looks east, a Bald Eagle's nest can be spotted.

Birds: Carlyle Lake is a magnet for migrating water birds — the biggest such magnet in our area, and the only large body of water for many miles in this part of Illinois. The water birds are supplemented by a fair assortment of woodland and brush birds, open-country raptors, and passerines in the surrounding farmland. The best birding occurs from mid-September through spring; the early-fall shorebird migration is usually not productive because good shorebird habitat is lacking.

During peaks of migration in the spring and fall, a wide variety of waterfowl use the lake and can be readily observed from points like Hickory Hollow (best in morning, with the sun behind you) or Hazlet State Park (best in afternoon for the same reason). Birds tend to congregate toward the center of the lake, beyond easy binocular range, so a spotting scope is almost essential. Flocks may include Canada, Snow, and perhaps Greater White-fronted Geese, Mallards and Lesser Scaup by the thousands, and dozens or so of Northern Pintail, American Wigeon, Ruddy Duck, Canvasback, mergansers, and other ducks. Common Loons and Horned Grebes are nearly always present in season, as are Double-crested Cormorants. The ubiquitous Ring-billed Gulls are joined by Herring Gulls, which increase in numbers as winter approaches. Bonaparte's and Franklin's Gulls plus Forster's and Caspian Terns are common as migrants.

Just as it attracts large and reliable numbers of commoner birds, Carlyle Lake also pulls in scarce and vagrant species with surprising regularity. While the likelihood of any particular rare species always remains low, the birder's chances of finding something unusual at Carlyle Lake are actually pretty good. Rarities found in recent years, many of them repeatedly or in multiples, include two species of loon (Red-throated and Pacific), four grebes (Eared, Red-necked, Western, and Clark's), Tundra Swans, various geese and ducks (e.g., Cinnamon Teal and all three scoters), Red Phalarope, Pomarine and Parasitic Jaegers, and a number of gulls. Of the latter, several tend to appear with cold weather (Thayer's, Great and Lesser Black-backed, Glaucous, and Black-legged Kittiwake) while others have appeared during the migration period (Laughing, Sabine's, Little, California). There is one record of Mew Gull. Rare sightings along the edge of the lake and on nearby farmland have included Black-throated Blue Warbler and Snow Bunting. In 1988 a Snowy Owl chose the marina area of Hazlet State Park as its winter quarters. In the winters of 1992 and 1993, Northern Saw-whet Owls roosted in red cedars at Hazlet State Park.

General Information: All posted park rules and regulations should be followed. Hunting is allowed in Hazlet State Park in the fall, and birders are advised to stay out. Boaters should take care as the lake contains tree stumps, boulders, and other debris. Restroom facilities can be found throughout the area. Camping is allowed in designated areas. Eating establishments and a few motels can be found in the town of Carlyle; additional motels can be found in the Vandalia area to the northeast on I-70.

BALDWIN LAKE   [X]
Randolph and St. Clair Counties, Illinois   *(Map 11)*

Attractions: Open water is guaranteed in winter. Baldwin Lake is the most reliable location in the area for Ross's Goose.

Directions: Baldwin Lake is located just north of Baldwin, Illinois, about 30 miles southeast of St. Louis. From loop freeway I-255 in East St. Louis, take IL-15 southeast. At Freeburg, IL-15 turns left (east) and IL-13 continues south (straight ahead). Go straight on IL-13 past New Athens to Baldwin Rd. (county highway R28, at the east edge of the town) and turn right (south); this intersection is 26.4 miles from I-255. Drive 5.3 miles to Risdon Road (county highway J42) and turn right (west) where a sign indicates the Kaskaskia River State Fish and Wildlife Area, which contains Baldwin Lake. The alternative route (shown on Map 11) is somewhat longer. After crossing the Mississippi River (on either I-55/I-64/I-70 or I-255), take IL-3 south. Continue south to Redbud and then take IL-154 about 7 miles east to Baldwin. Turn left (north) on county highway R28, drive about 3 miles north to Risdon Road, and turn left.

On returning to St. Louis from Baldwin Lake, go north on county highway R28, cross IL-13 into New Athens, and follow the signs to the *Peabody River King Fish and Wildlife Area* just east of town along the Kaskaskia River. This 2000-acre area is a reclaimed strip coal mine that was opened to the public in 1994. The area consists largely of ridges covered by short grass with deep intervening gullies and about 20 lakes and ponds. The full birding potential has yet to be discovered, but Short-eared Owls, Northern Harriers, and other raptors occur in winter.

Description: This 2,100-acre lake was created as a cooling "pond" for the coal-fired generators of the adjacent power plant. The discharge water is too warm to freeze in winter, thus providing an attractive oasis for wintering waterfowl. The area north and west of the power plant is managed by the Illinois Department of Conservation.

Best Sites: The gravel road south of the boat launch ramp and main parking lot provides a good view of the lake to the east. Fields on either side of the road usually contain feeding geese during the fall and winter. Birds can also be viewed from an observation platform on the south side of the parking lot.

Birds: A small flock of Canada Geese breeds here. In the fall, large flocks of Snow and Canada Geese arrive and use the lake as winter quarters. The Snow Goose flocks usually contain one or more of the rare Ross's Goose. (The lake is also home to a number of domestic geese.) The warm waters attract some species that seldom linger into winter elsewhere in the St. Louis area. These have included Common Loon, Horned and Eared Grebes, White-fronted Goose, Northern Pintail, Northern Shoveler, American Wigeon, Sandhill Crane (very rare), and Bonaparte's Gull. In 1987, a Brant was seen by many observers. Other birds found near the lake include Willow Flycatcher, Eastern Bluebird, Loggerhead Shrike, Lapland Longspur, and various sparrows.

General Information: The area is open 8:00 a.m. to 4:00 p.m. Pit toilets are available near the boat ramp. Hunting is not allowed on Baldwin Lake, but because adjacent areas along the Kaskaskia River are heavily hunted in fall, visitors should exercise care at this time of year. The hunting, however, does encourage birds to concentrate on the lake.

MONROE COUNTY LEVEE REGION [Y]
Monroe County, Illinois *(Maps 15 & 11)*

Attractions: The region of leveed Mississippi River floodplain south of St. Louis in Illinois provides good habitat for water-related birds during wet years. Extensive woodlands attract land birds, especially during migration.

Note: The flood of 1993 inundated all of the Monroe County flood-plain. Some roads shown on Map 15 were eroded, many homes were destroyed, and the town of Valmeyer was heavily damaged. At this writing, there are plans to move Valmeyer to higher ground. Therefore, all mention of "Valmeyer" here refers to the intersection of IL-156 and Bluff Road. The future status of local roads and smaller communities such as Fults is unknown at this writing.

Directions: From Missouri, take I-255 east over the Jefferson Barracks bridge, and continue about 2.5 miles to IL-3. Exit south on IL-3 toward Columbia. At the first stoplight (Sand Bank Road), turn right and descend down the steep hill to Bluff Road at the bottom of the bluff, about 0.3 miles. Turn left onto Bluff Road. After a mile you will cross a one-lane bridge and immediately after the bridge, Bluff Road takes a sharp right. Continue on Bluff Road 0.5 miles to Bottom Road, turn right, and drive 2 miles to the Levee Road. To reach a more central area, continue on IL-3 south of Columbia 7.6 miles to IL-156 at Waterloo. Turn right on IL-156, and drive 9.2 miles to Valmeyer. Continue on the road to the road atop the levee.

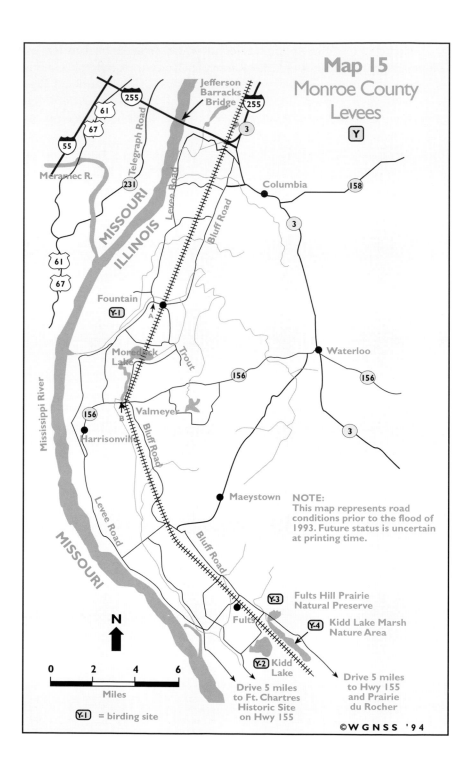

Map 15
Monroe County
Levees

Y

Jefferson
Barracks
Bridge

255

255

61

67

3

55

231

Columbia

158

Meramec R.

Telegraph Road

Levee Road

MISSOURI

ILLINOIS

3

61

67

Fountain

Y-1

A

Trout

Waterloo

Moredock
Lake

Bluff Road

156

156

Mississippi River

156

Valmeyer

3

B

Harrisonville

Bluff Road

Maeystown

NOTE:
This map represents road
conditions prior to the flood of
1993. Future status is uncertain
at printing time.

Levee Road

MISSOURI

Bluff Road

Y-3   Fults Hill Prairie
       Natural Preserve

Fults

Y-4   Kidd Lake Marsh
       Nature Area

N

Y-2   Kidd
       Lake

Drive 5 miles
to Hwy 155
and Prairie
du Rocher

0   2   4   6

Miles

Drive 5 miles
to Ft. Chartres
Historic Site
on Hwy 155

Y-1 = birding site

©WGNSS '94

Description: The floodplain varies in width from 2 to 5 miles and extends from I-255 south to the Kaskaskia River in Randolph County, although most birding is done in Monroe County. The Mississippi River forms the western boundary of the area and a wooded bluff forms the eastern boundary. A high levee with a road on top runs parallel to the river. Most of the floodplain is planted in row crops. During wet years, a series of sloughs and mudflats can be found along the river side of the levee.

Best Sites: The levee road south of I-255 provides access to the north levee region, which is good for herons and shorebirds during wet years. Stop at a creek, with an adjacent woods, about 3 miles south of I-255. This spot is especially good for spring migrants. Continue on Levee Road (not always on the levee) about 3 miles to *Fountain Creek* **[Y-1]**. Turn right, and follow the creek toward the Mississippi River. Look for herons and shorebirds along the way. The Levee Road turns south, and you can drive 20 miles to Fort de Chartres, checking the sloughs and woods along the way. There are several east-bound roads along the way on which you can return to Bluff Road.

As an alternative(↑A on Map 15), turn left at Fountain Creek for 0.6 miles, and turn right on Bluff Road. Continue south on Bluff Road 2 miles, and turn left onto Trout Road. The road winds its way up the bluff through a woods that is good for both breeding and migrant birds. Return to Bluff Road, turn left, and drive 4.5 miles to Valmeyer, checking Moredock Lake along the way. The lake has been good for herons, rails, and shorebirds. At Valmeyer(↑B on Map 15), you can either continue south on Bluff Road toward Fults, or turn right onto IL-156, and drive 4 miles to the Levee Road.

To reach *Kidd Lake* **[Y-2]** from Valmeyer, drive south on Bluff Road 12.4 miles (1.4 miles past the road to Fults), and turn right on Kidd Lake Road. Drive a short distance and park along the road just over the railroad tracks. Walk down the tracks for one view of the lake. For another view, drive 0.4 miles farther. In wet years, Kidd Lake is good for herons, waterfowl, shorebirds, and terns. To reach the Fort de Chartres Historic Site, continue about 1 mile to a crossroad, turn left, and drive 5 miles. This a good place to have a picnic lunch under the shade trees.

The *Fults Hill Prairie Nature Preserve* **[Y-3]** is located just south of Kidd Lake Road and on the left side (east) of Bluff Road. There is a small parking area. The rugged hills of this 532-acre natural area have forest, prairie, and limestone glade communities that attract a variety of breeding and migrant birds.

The 444-acre *Kidd Lake Marsh Nature Area* **[Y-4]** is located just south of the Fults Hill Prairie parking area and is between the Bluff Road and the railroad tracks. The best birding here is in spring for migrant marsh birds.

There are a number of side roads off Bluff and Levee Roads that are also worth exploring.

Birds: The levee region provides a good sample of breeding birds of the Mississippi River floodplain. Shrubby areas shelter Orchard Orioles and a few Blue Grosbeaks. Some of the fields may contain Dickcissels and Sedge Wrens. The extensive stands of tall cottonwoods along the river side of the levee have numbers of Northern Orioles and American Redstarts, as well as cuckoos, flycatchers, and other birds. Red-headed Woodpeckers are common throughout. Since there are fewer permanent sloughs and marshes than there used to be, water birds are harder to find, but the birder may still encounter both species of night-heron and all three egrets, if habitat is located.

Many rarities and "firsts" have occurred in Monroe County. The first Anhinga, Tricolored Heron, Scissor-tailed Flycatcher, and Fish Crow to be found in the St. Louis area were seen here, as were the first breeding Cattle Egrets and Mississippi Kites. A pair of possibly breeding Black-necked Stilts were found along Fountain Creek in 1993. Other rare or casual species seen here have included White, Glossy, and White-faced Ibises, Wood Stork, Brant, Black Vulture, and Purple Gallinule. Over thirty species of shorebirds, including Whimbrel, Hudsonian Godwit, and Buff-breasted Sandpiper, have been noted. Nearly all the warblers that pass through the area have been seen, including Black-throated Blue. It is possible to find 100 to 120 species in one day in this area during the spring migration.

General Information: This trip is extensive and will require a full day in order to enjoy the many birds. There are services available in Columbia and Waterloo.

FORT KASKASKIA HISTORICAL SITE [Z]
Randolph County, Illinois (Map 11)

Attractions: The small park at Fort Kaskaskia has consistently been host to nesting Mississippi Kites since they were first found there in 1962.

Directions: In Illinois, take IL-3 south from I-255 (about 2.5 miles east of the Jefferson Barracks bridge). After going south for 45 miles, turn right on Fort Kaskaskia Road, about 11 miles past IL-155 at Ruma. The park entrance is 1.5 miles west on the right.

Description: Only 275 acres in size, this compact park contains picnicking and camping facilities as well as a shelter and overlook on a high bluff above the Mississippi River and historic Kaskaskia Island, where the town of Kaskaskia once stood. Kaskaskia was the first capital of Illinois in 1818.

Best Sites: The overlook is the best spot to scan the river and the nearby second-growth woods. The elevation of this vantage point sometimes allows birders to enjoy a top view of Turkey Vultures and Mississippi Kites as they hunt back and forth. The adjoining road along the railroad tracks at the bottom of the bluff can also be productive.

Birds: Besides the graceful birds of prey mentioned above, Ruby-throated Hummingbird, Fish Crow, Summer Tanager, Blue Grosbeak, Chipping Sparrow, and Orchard Oriole can usually be found at or near the site.

General Information: The site is open year-round from 6 a.m. to 10 p.m. Toilets and drinking water are available. Campers need a permit from the site staff. The telephone number is (618) 859-3741.

Mississippi Kites

HABITAT INDEX FOR POPULAR BIRDING LOCATIONS

In the table below, some selected birding locations are grouped by type of habitat. The table can be correlated with Timetable for Birding Locations to select best months and types of birds to expect. Many of these locations have other types of habitat present. The locations are not ranked in order of preference. Mudflats and marshes vary greatly in quality with water levels.

LAKES	location	MUDFLATS	location
Riverlands EDA	[G]	Riverlands EDA	[G]
Horseshoe Lake	[U]	Marais Temps Clair	[J]
Carlyle Lake	[W]	Busch CA	[K]
Baldwin Lake	[X]	Clarence Cannon NWR	[M]
Mark Twain NWR	[S]	Horseshoe Lake	[U]
Swan Lake		Monroe County levees	[Y]
Stump Lake		Eagle Park marsh	[U]
Gilbert Lake		Hayford Road	[H]
Batchtown			
Winfield dam	[N]		

MARSHES		FORESTS & TREES	
Marais Temps Clair	[J]	Forest Park-Kennedy Forest	[A]
Riverlands EDA	[G]	Tower Grove Park	[B]
Mark Twain NWR	[S]	Busch CA	[K]
Stump Lake		Pere Marquette State Park	[R]
Gilbert Lake		Shaw Arboretum	[O]
Horseshoe Lake	[U]	Creve Coeur Park	[C]
Eagle Park marsh	[U]	Gilbert Lake	[S]
Moredock Lake	[Y]		

OPEN WATER DURING SEVERE WINTERS

Artificially Warmed		*Below Dams*	
Dresser Island access	[H]	Winfield dam, No. 25	[N]
Horseshoe Lake	[U]	Melvin Price dam, No. 26R	[G]
IL-143, Alton		Chain-of-Rocks dam, No. 27	[T]
power plant pond	[T]	Lock No. 27 (Granite City)	[T]
Baldwin Lake	[X]	Carlyle Lake dam	[W]

A TIMETABLE FOR BIRDING LOCATIONS

The following timetable indicates which groups of birds are best represented at major birding areas during each month of the year. Groups in parentheses are of secondary importance.

Location	Jan	Feb	Mar	Apr	May	Jun	Jul	Aug	Sep	Oct	Nov	Dec
Forest Park				LB	LB				LB	LB		
Tower Grove Park				LB	LB (SP)				LB	LB (SP)	LB	
Shaw Arboretum	WF	WF		LB (SP)	LB	LB		LB	LB	LB		WF
Busch CA	LB BP	LB WB	LB WB	LB	LB (SB)	LB		LB	LB BP	LB WB	LB WB	LB WB
St. Charles Airport	GFB	GFB	GFB	SB	SB				GFB	GFB	GFB	GFB
Marais Temps Clair	BP	WB	WB	WB LW R	LW R				LW (R)	WB	WB BP	BP WB
Riverlands & Melvin Price Dam	WB G BP	WB G	WB G	SB G/T R	SB T R	LW	LW	SB T LW	SB T LW	WB G/T SB	WB G BP	WB G BP
Mississippi River	WB G	WB G	WB G	WB G/T		T			WB T	WB G/T	WB G	WB G
Mark Twain NWR	BP WB	BP WB	WB BP LB	WB SB	SB LB		(LW)	SB LW (WB)	LB LW	WB LB	WB BP	WB BP
Pere Marquette State Park	BP (WF)			LB	LB	LB			LB	LB	BP	BP (WF)
Horseshoe Lake	G WB	WB (SP)	WB SP	WB LB SP	LB WB T	R LW	SB LW	SB LW	SB T LW	WB SP (G)	WB SP G	WB G
Carlyle Lake & Dam	G WB GFB	WB G GFB	WB	WB LB T	LB WB T		(SB)	(SB)	LB T (SB)	WB G/T LB	WB G	WB G GFB

BP ... Birds of Prey (vultures, hawks, kites, eagles, falcons)
G .... Gulls
GFB .. Grassy Field Birds (longspurs, pipits, larks, etc.)
LB ... Landbirds (woodpeckers, flycatchers, warblers, thrushes, etc.)
LW... Large Waders (herons, egrets, bitterns, ibises)
R .... Rails (rails, gallinules, coots)
SB.... Shorebirds (plovers, sandpipers, phalaropes)
SP.... Sparrows
T .... Terns
WB... Waterbirds (loons, grebes, cormorants, ducks, geese)
WF... Winter Finches (crossbills, finches, siskins)

Eastern Screech-Owl

SPECIES ACCOUNTS

his chapter provides information about the best habitat and most likely localities to find each of the bird species that regularly occur in the St. Louis area. In addition, for species that are *Extinct* or *Extirpated* from the area, information is provided about their prior occurrence. For species having less than five records in any season, i.e., those designated *Accidental* on the **SEASONAL OCCURRENCE** bar graphs, the dates and location (if known) of each record are discussed. For many species, the date and place of the first sighting are also given. The information presented here is current as of December, 1993. In total, 370 species are discussed.

Species designated *Hypothetical* are those for which there is at least one credible report, often by a single observer, but for which there is no specimen, acceptable photograph, or corroborating observations. For some *Hypothetical* species, there are several reports, but the records have not been accepted by the Missouri or Illinois bird records committees. They are included for information only, with hope that further information or future sightings can confirm the occurrence of the species in our area.

Because information on the relative abundance and the best time of year to see each species is provided in the **SEASONAL OCCURRENCE** bar graphs, such information is generally not repeated here. For some species, however, high counts or typical numbers at the peak of occurrence are given. Information available in field guides on field marks and behavior is generally not discussed here unless it is particularly relevant to local identification problems.

The order in which species are presented follows that of the 1983 *A.O.U. Checklist* (A.O.U., 1983). Both common and scientific names are current as of the *39th Supplement* to the *Checklist*. This includes the retrograde name changes of Green-backed Heron to Green Heron and Lesser Golden-Plover to American Golden-Plover.

Sources of Information. The information provided in this chapter and in the chapter on **SEASONAL OCCURRENCE** is based largely on observations of many area birders recorded in *Nature Notes*, the journal of the Webster Groves Nature Study Society. It is also based on personal notes of the authors and other contributors regarding their own observations and the observations of others. Some information from *The Birds of Illinois* by Bohlen and Zimmerman (1989) and *Birds of Missouri* by Robbins and Easterla (1992) is reviewed. The historical information is based on *A Preliminary Catalog of the Birds of Missouri* by Otto Widmann (1907) and the Hurter collection.

Hurter Bird Collection. Julius Hurter was born in 1842, educated in Switzerland, and employed as a mechanical engineer in Paris, France, before moving to the United States in 1865. He settled in St. Louis in 1866 and worked for 40 years at the Fulton Iron Co. as an engineer and chief draftsman. Hurter had an interest in nature and was eager to collect and preserve specimens of birds, reptiles, and amphibians. His herpetology collection of 3,575 specimens was donated to the U. S. National Museum after his death in 1916. His collection of 284 bird specimens collected near St. Louis in Illinois and Missouri was eventually turned over to Washington University. The collection was housed at the Masonic Temple on Lindell Boulevard until 1945. During this time several specimens such as Carolina Parakeet and Passenger Pigeon disappeared. Art students had access to the collection and "borrowed" some of the specimens for models which apparently did not fly back. In 1945 Washington University arranged to have the collection moved to the St. Louis Academy of Science, where it was housed for many years. Presently, the collection is curated by the St. Louis Science Center.

LOONS AND GREBES

Red-throated Loon *(Gavia stellata).* Since this species was first found in our area in 1942, there have been 20 records. Seventeen are from the fall season; all of these have been of single birds, mostly juveniles. The rest are spring records: 21 March 1962 (Holten State Park), 8 April 1976 (Horseshoe Lake), and 11-12 March 1988 (Horseshoe Lake).

Pacific Loon *(Gavia pacifica).* There have been about nine records of the species since it was first discovered in our area in 1984. All are from Horseshoe Lake, Carlyle Lake, and the Riverlands/Alton area. Most birds were juveniles and occurred singly.

Common Loon *(Gavia immer)*. This large loon is most easily observed during fall migration. A few individuals linger until forced out by ice; the artificially warmed waters of Baldwin Lake provide the only consistent source for early winter sightings. Although the species can be found on any large body of water, Horseshoe Lake, Swan Lake, Carlyle Lake, and the Riverlands/Alton area have been the most reliable places.

Pied-billed Grebe *(Podilymbus podiceps)*. Pied-billed Grebes are found on ponds, lakes and marshes. Breeding occurs in shallow marshes with some open water. Recent breeding sites include Marais Temps Clair, Eagle Park marsh, Clarence Cannon NWR, and Riverlands EDA.

Horned Grebe *(Podiceps auritus)*. This grebe prefers larger bodies of water than the Pied-billed Grebe. It is not uncommon to see 30-70 individuals at the peak of fall migration, and a high number of about 150 has been recorded. Substantial numbers gather at Baldwin Lake after other areas have frozen; over 70 individuals have been seen in January. Other good locations are Carlyle Lake, Swan Lake, Horseshoe Lake, and Riverlands EDA. During March and April this species undergoes a molt, producing some intermediate plumages that are easily confused with those of the Eared Grebe. There is one summer record: 13 June 1971 (Randolph Co.)

Red-necked Grebe *(Podiceps grisegena)*. All records except one are of single birds. There have been six spring, eleven fall, and one winter occurrence, including unusual dates of 31 December 1949 (Horseshoe Lake), 27 May 1984 (Marais Temps Clair), and 13-19 March 1993 (Riverlands EDA). Several of the fall migrants have remained for several days. Seek this species in areas where loons and other grebes congregate.

Eared Grebe *(Podiceps nigricollis)*. Although most regularly found on large bodies of water (Carlyle, Baldwin, Creve Coeur, and Swan Lakes, and Lake 33 at Busch CA), this species has also been found on shallow sewage lagoons and ponds (Mueller Road, Carlyle, and O'Fallon, Illinois). Most records involve only one or two birds. All winter records are from Baldwin Lake. There is one summer record: 5-12 June 1983 (Eagle Park marsh).

Western Grebe *(Aechmophorus occidentalis)*. There are fourteen fall and two spring records for our area, although some of these may have been Clark's Grebes, as no report of "Western Grebe" prior to 1983 includes sufficient detail to differentiate between this and the next species.

The spring sightings occurred on 10 April 1982 (Horseshoe Lake) and 5 May 1991 (Busch CA); there is also an early fall sighting of a bird that lingered from 6 September to 13 October 1973 (Swan Lake). Nearly all records are from the large lakes: Carlyle, Swan, Horseshoe, Busch CA, and Riverlands/Alton. Only three of the records involved multiple individuals, with a high of six birds on 5 December 1982 (Carlyle Lake).

Clark's Grebe *(Aechmophorus clarkii)*. This species was officially recognized by the A. O. U. in 1985; prior to that it was regarded as a color morph of the Western Grebe. There have been three records for our area: a single bird, 24 November to 14 December 1983 (Horseshoe Lake), two birds, 11 October 1992 (Carlyle Lake), and a single bird, 18-23 November 1993 (Carlyle Lake).

Mounted specimen of Band-rumped Storm-Petrel

STORM-PETREL, PELICAN, CORMORANTS, AND ANHINGA

Band-rumped Storm-Petrel *(Oceanodroma castro)*. An exhausted individual of this species was found on a farm in Defiance (St. Charles Co.) on 2 September 1950. The bird was identified as "Madeira Petrel" (a former name of O. *castro*) by local birders, who took measurements that were sent to an unidentified museum ornithologist who confirmed the identification. The mounted specimen was lost for several years (Robbins and Easterla, 1992) but was rediscovered in 1994 in the collection of the St. Louis Science Center, where the identification was reconfirmed (Anderson, 1994). The arrival of this Atlantic ocean bird may have been assisted by Hurricane Baker, which came ashore at Mobile, Alabama on 30 August 1950, proceeded north as a tropical storm to near Memphis, Tennessee on 1 September, and passed through the St. Louis area just before the bird was discovered.

American White Pelican *(Pelecanus erythrorhynchos)*. This species has been observed regularly in the fall at Swan Lake in numbers sometimes exceeding 100, but only infrequently elsewhere. In the fall of 1992, however, there were several reports from Horseshoe Lake, Creve Coeur Lake, Riverlands EDA, and the Winfield dam. Small flocks have been seen overhead in fall by observers at hawk lookouts. There are occasional records during July and August of visitors that have lingered for weeks. Overwintering birds have probably been sick or injured, although a flock of 20 healthy birds was seen as late as 18 December in 1993.

Double-crested Cormorant *(Phalacrocorax auritus)*. By the early 1970's, cormorants had been reduced to uncommon migrants in our area, probably as a result of habitat loss, persecution, and pesticides. Since then, they have staged a dramatic recovery. Currently, during the spring and fall migrations, it is easy to find hundreds on larger lakes or rivers, especially Riverlands EDA and Carlyle, Swan, and Horseshoe Lakes. In the early 1990's, breeding was reestablished in the area (Carlyle Lake, Kidd Lake).

Neotropic Cormorant *(Phalacrocorax brasilianus)*. There is only one record for this Gulf Coast species, a single bird with a flock of about 300 Double-crested Cormorants, 30 August to 12 September 1992 at Riverlands EDA. It was seen by many observers and photographed.

Anhinga *(Anhinga anhinga)*. The area's first Anhinga was seen and photographed at Fountain Creek in Monroe Co. on 21-23 July 1993.

BITTERNS, HERONS, EGRETS, AND NIGHT-HERONS

American Bittern *(Botaurus lentiginosus)*. Finding this shy bird usually requires a deliberate search of large cattail marshes; particularly cooperative birds can sometimes be found "frozen" at the edge of a marsh. For the best chance, one should walk the dikes at Marais Temps Clair in early morning during spring migration. Vocalizations are given only infrequently in this area. There are two single-bird winter records: 28 January 1971 (St. Charles Co.) and 8 November to 31 December 1991 (Riverlands EDA).

Least Bittern *(Ixobrychus exilis)*. This bittern is found in a wider variety of marsh habitat than the preceding species; however, the best locality is Marais Temps Clair, where it nests regularly. Other localities, depending on seasonal rainfall and water levels, include Horseshoe Lake (south of causeway and at Eagle Park marsh) and Riverlands EDA (Teal Pond). The status of the species in our area during fall migration is not well known and needs study.

Great Blue Heron *(Ardea herodias)*. This large heron should be a familiar sight to anyone frequenting wetlands. It is especially abundant in the Mississippi and Illinois River floodplains. In winter, it occurs near open water along the rivers and at Horseshoe and Swan Lakes; as many as 50 birds have been counted in some locations. Breeding occurs in colonies on wooded islands in the major rivers.

Great Blue Heron

Great Egret *(Casmerodius albus)*. This species is almost entirely restricted to wetlands in the floodplains of the Mississippi, Missouri, Illinois, and Kaskaskia Rivers, especially during late spring and early summer. In late summer, concentrations of over 100 birds can be found.

Snowy Egret *(Egretta thula)*. Sightings for spring and early summer are usually from Horseshoe Lake and Riverlands EDA. Some of the birds come from Madison and St. Clair Co. nesting colonies, which have contained as many as 20 nesting pairs and are the only known breeding locations in our area. As with the Great Egret, in late summer the local population is augmented by post-breeding dispersal into this area of young birds from southern populations.

Little Blue Heron *(Egretta caerulea).* Most sightings occur in the Mississippi River floodplain around Horseshoe Lake or in St. Charles County. Nesting colonies near Horseshoe Lake contain the northernmost nesting population of this species in Illinois, often numbering around 100 pairs. Late summer concentrations have produced counts of over 400 at Horseshoe Lake.

Tricolored Heron *(Egretta tricolor).* Sightings of this southern heron have occurred in eight different years beginning in 1968; all have been of single birds. None of the birds has appeared to be immature and no nesting has been discovered or suspected. Thus, most occurrences are probably of non-breeding adults, in contrast to the usual pattern of northern records of southern herons in Illinois. Subadult Little Blue Herons can resemble and be misidentified as Tricolored Herons.

[Reddish Egret *(Egretta rufescens)***]** *Hypothetical.* There have been three reports of single birds, all by single observers: 29 July 1949 (Chain of Rocks), 30 September 1951 (Marais Temps Clair), and 25 June 1972 (Monroe Co., near the bridge at Jefferson Barracks).

Cattle Egret *(Bubulcus ibis).* This small egret colonized North America from Africa via northern South America, the Caribbean, and then Florida. It first appeared in our area in 1955 but was not regularly seen until 1962. It is commonly found at Holten State Park and Riverlands EDA. It has bred at Horseshoe Lake and other locations in the Mississippi River floodplain of Illinois.

Green Heron *(Butorides virescens).* This small heron prefers bodies of water bordered by trees or shrubs with overhanging branches. It does not congregate in nesting colonies to breed as do the larger herons. It is often found on streams like the Meramec River and small ponds like the lagoons of Forest Park. There are two winter records, both from the Orchard Farm (St. Charles Co.) Christmas Bird Count: 19-25 December 1980 and 2 January 1983.

Black-crowned Night-Heron *(Nycticorax nycticorax).* Although this species has declined in numbers over the past fifty years, it has recovered slightly since 1970. It is most commonly found at Horseshoe Lake, but also at Riverlands EDA and Marais Temps Clair. In summer, Black-crowns are often seen in various parts of the metropolitan area flying to feeding areas at dusk. In winter, birds are sometimes found at Horseshoe and Swan Lakes. A Black-crowned nesting colony near Horseshoe Lake in the 1980's was probably the largest in Illinois, with as many as 200 nests.

Yellow-crowned Night-Heron *(Nyctanassa violacea)*. The Black-crowned feeds mainly on fish while the Yellow-crowned thrives on crayfish, so it is not surprising that the two night-herons are not often found-together. Yellow-crowned Night-Herons occur around Horseshoe Lake but are most reliably found near Holten State Park and in Calhoun Co. (both areas are near breeding sites).

IBISES, SPOONBILL, AND STORK

White Ibis *(Eudocimus albus)*. There is a total of eleven records of this species, and ten of these have occurred since 1962. There are only three spring records, all of single adults: 23 May 1964 (Moredock Lake), 4 May 1985 (Horseshoe Lake), and 15 April 1992 (Madison Co). All but one of the late summer and fall records are of juveniles.

Glossy Ibis *(Plegadis falcinellus)*. The two species of *Plegadis* ibis are difficult to distinguish in the field, and both are out of their normal range in St. Louis. The seven records of dark ibises positively identified as Glossy have all occurred in the spring. There are four spring and three fall records for which details are insufficient to distinguish between the two species; these are indicated as "*Plegadis* sp.?" on the **SEASONAL OCCURRENCE** bar graphs.

White-faced Ibis *(Plegadis chihi)*. There have been about 15 verified records of this species since 1978, nearly all in spring (see preceding species). Only two dark ibises observed in fall, both adults, have been observed closely enough to be positively identified as White-faced: 30 August 1981 (present Riverlands EDA location) and 10-22 September 1983 (Centreville, Illinois). Most sightings have come from St. Charles Co., and at least four records are of multiple individuals, including a flock of seven.

[Roseate Spoonbill *(Ajaia ajaja)***]** *Hypothetical.* The only report of this southern species was given by Ridgway (1895), who indicated that a taxidermist had shot several specimens near some ponds in the Mississippi River bottoms below St. Louis in about 1859 (see Bohlen and Zimmerman, 1989). There is also a specimen with no accompanying data in the Hurter collection.

Wood Stork *(Mycteria americana)*. When Wood Storks had a larger breeding range in the south, they were fairly regular post-breeding visitors to our area, with as many as 130 birds observed on 24 August 1932. However, since 1940 they have only been recorded three times: 16-26 July 1952 in Seckman (Jefferson Co.), 26 August 1952 at Horseshoe Lake, and a flock of 23 immature birds on 8 August 1963 near Fults (Monroe Co.).

WATERFOWL

The numbers of migrating ducks and geese vary considerably from year to year, primarily because of variation in the availability of suitable nesting habitat north of St. Louis. It is encouraging that new wetlands are being created locally to furnish accommodations for migrating or wintering waterfowl. The numbers of wintering ducks depend on the severity of the winter and availability of open water.

Fulvous Whistling-Duck *(Dendrocygna bicolor)*. One sighting of two birds seen in a drainage canal near Horseshoe Lake on 2 September 1933 remains the only record of this species. Two birds were found and photographed just north of the St. Louis area at Ted Shanks CA, 2-21 June 1981.

[Black-bellied Whistling-Duck *(Dendrocygna autumnalis)*] *Hypothetical.* Eighteen birds were reported at a hunting club west of Portage Des Sioux, 18-25 October 1989.

Tundra Swan *(Cygnus columbianus)*. This species is most often found at Mark Twain NWR. Most observations are of one or two birds that remain for more than a week. A large flock of about 18 was found in Randolph Co. on 26 March 1979.

Mute Swan *(Cygnus olor)* **Introduced.** Mute Swans can be found unrestrained on ponds associated with private estates or collections, so when one is seen in some unexpected area it is often difficult to determine whether it is a local escapee or a truly wild bird from the Great Lakes population. A pair of birds seen on Alton Lake on 7-10 January 1984 and again between 6 January and 7 February in 1985 were probably true vagrants rather than local escapees.

Trumpeter Swan *(Cygnus buccinator)* **Extirpated.** A fairly common breeder in our area up until the late 1800's, this species almost became extinct around 1912. Conservation efforts in the west have been successful, and now the species is no longer considered endangered nationally. In the 1980's, reintroduction programs began in Wisconsin and Michigan, and in November 1991, descendants of these transplants began to appear in the St. Louis area in early winter, usually in eastern St. Charles Co. Although the situation is encouraging, the birds are not really wild. Colored neck bands and aluminum leg bands provide ways to track and identify these rather tame offspring.

Greater White-fronted Goose *(Anser albifrons)*. Because St. Louis is east of this species' main migration route, it is usually found only in small flocks during migration. It is reported annually from Busch CA, Mark Twain NWR, and Carlyle Lake, where it is usually seen mixed with flocks of Canada Geese. Most winter records are of one or two birds.

Snow Goose *(Chen caerulescens)*. Two large wintering flocks located within our area represent the northern limit of this species' wintering range on the Mississippi flyway. One flock, which has numbered as high as 15,000 birds, is found at the Mark Twain NWR or across the Mississippi River feeding in St. Charles Co. The other occurs at Baldwin Lake, where its peak numbers approach 5,000 birds. The blue morph, formerly regarded as a separate species, usually outnumbers the nominate white morph.

Ross's Goose *(Chen rossii)*. This goose was first identified in our area in 1951 and has been seen regularly since the 1980's. It is usually found in small numbers (1-6) in flocks of wintering Snow Geese, especially at Baldwin Lake, but also at Mark Twain NWR and in St. Charles Co.

Brant *(Branta bernicla)*. The eastern form of this species has been recorded four times: 9 November 1964 (shot on the Illinois River), 3-6 May 1968 (Monroe Co.), 31 October to 11 November 1978 (Mark Twain NWR), and 29 March to 4 April 1987 (Baldwin Lake).

[Barnacle Goose *(Branta leucopsis)*] **Hypothetical.** There is one record of this species, of an individual seen by several observers at Marais Temps Clair on 26 March 1950. Since this species breeds in Greenland and is commonly raised in captivity, most reports from the midwest are probably not of wild birds.

Canada Goose *(Branta canadensis)*. When St. Louis was first settled, the giant Canada Goose was a common nester along the bluffs of the

Mississippi and Missouri Rivers. However, as late as the early 1900's the Canada Goose was reduced to a common transient and uncommon winter resident. Around 1950 it began to reappear as a breeding species, almost coinciding with the creation of Busch CA. It has learned to coexist with man and has become a common nester. It is found throughout the year on nearly every pond and lake, sometimes in residential areas.

Wood Duck *(Aix sponsa)*. This beautiful bird, our most common nesting duck, is found in river bottomlands and swamps. The squeal-like alarm call given by the hen when startled into flight is a certain give-away of its presence. The lagoons of Forest Park are one of the most reliable places to observe this bird, which regularly nests in trees of the Kennedy Forest.

Green-winged Teal *(Anas crecca)*. This teal is observed during migration at the edge of ponds and lakes or in flooded fields. Look for it at Mark Twain NWR, Marais Temps Clair, and Riverlands EDA.

American Black Duck *(Anas rubripes)*. Black Ducks no longer occur in numbers as large as in the past. They are usually found in the company of Mallards at Carlyle Lake, Mark Twain NWR, Marais Temps Clair, and Riverlands EDA.

Mallard *(Anas platyrhynchos)*. This is our most common wintering duck, found in numbers ranging from a single pair to several thousand. Some Mallards stay to nest in our area. Sometimes it is difficult to determine whether a Mallard is wild, feral or domestic; if it has typical plumage and flies upon approach, it is probably wild.

Northern Pintail *(Anas acuta)*. This duck is usually found in the company of other puddle ducks. Once the water in shallow feeding areas freezes, the Pintail heads south, only to return quickly upon the resumption of mild weather. It appears to be decreasing in numbers.

Northern Pintail

Blue-winged Teal *(Anas discors)*. The Blue-wing is a common migrant, peaking later in spring and earlier in fall than most ducks. Although it has been observed throughout the summer, there have been only two nesting records. The only winter sightings are from the warm waters of Baldwin Lake or some protected pocket of a slough during a mild winter.

Cinnamon Teal *(Anas cyanoptera)*. Most sightings of this western species have been of males in spring; only two have occurred in fall: one bird, 28 October 1971 (Busch CA); and two birds, 18 September 1987 (Hawthorne Street).

Northern Shoveler *(Anas clypeata)*. Shovelers prefer shallow water and are sometimes found wading in water not deep enough to allow swimming. Before 1970, it was unusual to find Shovelers in winter; now they occur regularly if shallow, open water remains.

Gadwall *(Anas strepera)*. Gadwall are hardy and are sometimes found throughout winter at such places as Teal Pond at Riverlands EDA. In migration they can be found in any area with a concentration of puddle ducks.

Eurasian Wigeon *(Anas penelope)*. There are five records, all of single birds: 10 April 1905 (exact location unknown), 25-26 April 1943 and 23 March 1949 (both at Marais Temps Clair), 30 March 1969 (Stump Lake), and 10 November 1946 (St. Charles Co.). See Robbins and Easterla (1992).

American Wigeon *(Anas americana)*. This species can be found in flocks of more than 50 during migration, especially on large shallow lakes such as Swan Lake. Wintering birds are usually found one or two at a time.

Canvasback *(Aythya valisineria)*. This duck is usually restricted to large bodies of water. Most wintering Canvasbacks are found along the Mississippi River above the Alton dam; by early spring, rafts of hundreds can be found on the river. Birds sometimes linger into early summer, as evidenced by a female with five young at Horseshoe Lake on 4 May 1963.

Redhead *(Aythya americana)*. Redheads are usually found mixed with scaup and Canvasbacks, not in large flocks of their own species. Two summered at Eagle Park marsh in 1983, but there was no evidence of nesting.

Ring-necked Duck *(Aythya collaris)*. Although this diving duck bears a superficial resemblance to scaup, the Ring-neck is usually found in shallow water with dabbling ducks, rather than the deep water preferred by scaup. It is seen in numbers up to 50 on area lakes and rivers.

[Tufted Duck *(Aythya fuligula)***]** *Hypothetical.* There is one report of a female from Alton Lake, 4 April 1987.

Greater Scaup *(Aythya marila)*. This difficult-to-identify species occurs in smaller numbers than the Lesser Scaup, and less regularly. Sometimes the two scaup are found together, making the Greater easier to identify. It is usually seen at Riverlands EDA, Alton Lake, Horseshoe Lake, and sometimes on sewage lagoons.

Lesser Scaup *(Aythya affinis)*. This scaup often occurs in large flocks on open water. The largest flocks, sometimes numbering in the thousands, are found on Swan Lake and above the dams on the Mississippi River and Carlyle Lake.

King Eider *(Somateria spectabilis)*. Only one record exists, a specimen of an immature female found in the Hurter collection dated 24 November 1875 from Horseshoe Lake. The original label on the specimen was "Surf Scoter," but this was corrected in 1973 when the collection was reviewed.

Harlequin Duck *(Histrionicus histrionicus)*. The Hurter Collection contained a specimen (now missing) shot in St. Charles Co. on 29 October, sometime prior to 1884. This remains the only record for our area.

Oldsquaw *(Clangula hyemalis)*. The Oldsquaw is found almost every year at Alton and Carlyle Lakes and Riverlands EDA. It has also been seen on small ponds such as sewage lagoons or settling basins. Although sometimes found in small flocks, single birds are most often reported.

Black Scoter *(Melanitta nigra)*. This species is the least often observed of the three scoters. There are only a few records of adult males. One remarkable record exists of 3 males and 24 females at the Alton dam on 15 November 1977. It is most often seen on Alton, Horseshoe, Carlyle, and Swan Lakes.

Surf Scoter *(Melanitta perspicillata)*. There is only one modern spring record for this species: a female, 8 April 1972 (Alton dam). All other records are females or immatures found in the fall. The best locations are Alton Lake, Carlyle Lake, Riverlands EDA, and the O'Fallon (Illinois) sewage lagoon.

White-winged Scoter *(Melanitta fusca)*. This scoter has been recorded almost annually on large lakes such as Carlyle and Horseshoe, and on the Mississippi River.

Common Goldeneye *(Bucephala clangula)*. This duck can be found along the Mississippi River in winter as long as a single patch of open water remains. The noise of its whistling wings quickly helps identify the small compact flocks flying up or down the river. It is also found on other area rivers and lakes.

Barrow's Goldeneye *(Bucephala islandica)*. Although Widmann (1907) mentions a bird taken near St. Louis, there is no date or location known for the specimen. Four additional records are acknowledged: a juvenile male, 29-30 March 1947 (St. Charles Co.); a male, 13 December 1963 (Mark Twain NWR); a male, 16 January 1973, that remained for almost two weeks (Alton dam); and a female, 8 January 1977 (Chain of Rocks).

Bufflehead *(Bucephala albeola)*. Buffleheads are found on almost any size body of water and appear to be increasing in numbers. Flocks of up to 50 birds are not unusual.

Hooded Merganser *(Lophodytes cucullatus)*. This merganser can be seen on any area lake with concentrations of ducks; Riverlands EDA is a good place to seek it. A high count of around 300 occurred on 21 November 1987. Several females with young were observed at Clarence Cannon NWR in 1992 and 1993.

Common Merganser *(Mergus merganser)*. The Mississippi River between St. Louis and Keokuk, Iowa, is one of the major wintering areas for this species, and flocks of hundreds have been seen on Alton Lake. It is also common at Carlyle, Swan, and Horseshoe Lakes.

Red-breasted Merganser *(Mergus serrator)*. This species is more common some years than others during spring migration. The first fall migrants are usually females and immatures. It is best found at Horseshoe and Carlyle Lakes, Riverlands EDA, and Mark Twain NWR. There are two summer records of non-breeding females: 13 August 1973 (levee region) and 15 July through 23 August 1978 (Horseshoe Lake).

Ruddy Duck

Ruddy Duck *(Oxyura jamaicensis)*. This little duck is often observed in flocks of more than 100 in both shallow and deep water such as at Riverlands EDA or Carlyle Lake. Numbers seem to have declined during the 1980's. Adults with young were observed at Eagle Park marsh in 1983.

DIURNAL RAPTORS

Of the nineteen species of vulture, kite, eagle, hawk, and falcon that regularly occur in the St. Louis area, nine regularly breed. During the spring and fall migrations, hawk sightings can occur almost anywhere. However, certain geographic features like bluffs, ridges, and large bodies of water tend to concentrate migrating hawks so that the probability of seeing them some places is higher than others. Some known locations are the west shore of Carlyle Lake, Busch CA, and the hills near the Tyson Research Center.

Black Vulture *(Coragyps atratus)*. There are ten records for the area. The one Missouri record is from 26 April 1970 (Shaw Arboretum). All other records come from the levee region of Monroe County, except the most recent occurrence on 26 April 1984 from Horseshoe Lake.

Turkey Vulture *(Cathartes aura)*. Although it can be found anywhere during migration, the Turkey Vulture is most often seen along the Mississippi River bluffs or in the Ozarks in the southwest part of our area.

Osprey *(Pandion haliaetus)*. During the DDT era, the Osprey was dangerously low in numbers, but since the ban on DDT in 1972, it has recovered satisfactorily. Now, from 5 to 15 birds can be found in a day's search during the peak fall migration. It is most commonly seen at Busch CA, Riverlands EDA, and Mark Twain NWR. It once nested in this area, but no record exists since the 1800's. There have been two winter sightings: 15 February 1975 from Busch CA and 3 January 1980 at Marais Temps Clair.

Swallow-tailed Kite *(Elanoides forficatus)* **Extirpated**. Although it bred near St. Louis in the 1800's, this southern species has been long extirpated from our area. However, there have been recent sightings from other areas of Missouri and Illinois.

Mississippi Kite *(Ictinia mississippiensis)*. The first area record was at Pere Marquette State Park on the unusual date of 22 September 1956. In 1962 the kite was discovered nesting near Fults in Monroe Co. Since then it has been a regular summer resident along the Mississippi River in the southernmost part of our area (near Ft. Kaskaskia). Since the late 1980's it has nested in residential areas of St. Louis Co. (University City and Webster Groves) and is now routinely reported flying over the suburbs in summer.

Bald Eagle *(Haliaeetus leucocephalus)*. The Mississippi and Illinois Rivers north of St. Louis have some of the highest numbers of wintering Bald Eagles in the Midwest. Eagles are usually found stationed in large trees along the rivers or perched on ice near open water. After years of speculation that the Eagle might return as a nester, three nests were found within our area in 1992 (Clarence Cannon NWR, Slim Island in the Mississippi River, and Carlyle Lake). A high number of 307 was seen on an eagle count taken on 21 February 1970, and 180 were seen at Riverlands EDA on 8 January 1993.

Northern Harrier *(Circus cyaneus)*. This hawk is often found cruising low over marshlands or prairies, sometimes in pairs. More brown females and russet-bellied immatures are found than gray, adult males. They are most often seen in St. Charles Co.; Riverlands EDA has been an especially reliable spot. There are several old breeding records from St. Charles Co., but recent summer sightings are probably of nonbreeding birds.

Sharp-shinned Hawk *(Accipiter striatus)*. High counts for this migrant accipiter are 122 for Busch CA and 177 for Carlyle Lake, both on 4 October 1986. Although it is a rare breeder elsewhere in Illinois and Missouri, it is not known to nest within the St. Louis area. In winter, it is a regular resident of wooded areas in small numbers, but furtive and hard to observe. Both the Sharp-shinned and Cooper's Hawks are sometimes seen in the suburbs and occasionally dine on small birds visiting feeders.

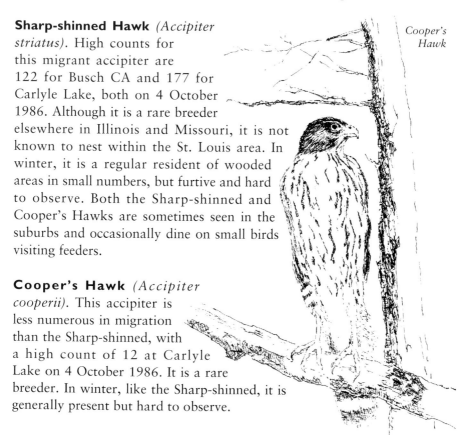

Cooper's Hawk

Cooper's Hawk *(Accipiter cooperii)*. This accipiter is less numerous in migration than the Sharp-shinned, with a high count of 12 at Carlyle Lake on 4 October 1986. It is a rare breeder. In winter, like the Sharp-shinned, it is generally present but hard to observe.

Northern Goshawk *(Accipiter gentilis)*. Although a resident of conifer-dominated woodlands in the north, the goshawk has been recorded locally in open farm country and even in Tower Grove Park. It is erratic in appearance this far south; the last two impressive invasions occurred in 1972-73 and 1982-83.

Red-shouldered Hawk *(Buteo lineatus)*. Once a fairly common resident of wooded riparian areas prior to the use of DDT, this hawk has never recovered its original numbers despite the ban on the pesticide. It can usually be found year-round at Shaw Arboretum and Tyson Research Center and is occasionally seen in migration.

Broad-winged Hawk *(Buteo platypterus)*. This species is often found in large numbers during migration. In fall, the majority of birds may pass through on a single day, and flocks of a hundred birds are sometimes seen circling over the suburbs. Broad-wings often migrate so high that they cannot be seen without binoculars. High numbers are 572 for spring (22 April 1990, Busch CA) and 5,419 for fall (4 October 1986, Jefferson Co.). The extreme early date is 10 March 1980, at Busch CA. A few nest locally in mature forests.

Swainson's Hawk *(Buteo swainsoni)*. There have been about 23 reports of this western hawk since 1949, 19 since 1970. Inasmuch as this species has an isolated nesting population in northern Illinois, it should be found regularly during migration; seek it in flocks of migrating Broad-wings.

Red-tailed Hawk *(Buteo jamaicensis)*. The Red-tail is by far the most common large hawk in our area. Local resident birds of the eastern race, which are fairly uniform in appearance, are augmented in fall and winter by an influx of birds from farther north and west, which are more variable in plumage — pale, rufous, dark, and "normal." In particular, the blackish Harlan's form, once considered a separate species, occurs here in small numbers from November through March, and must be separated with care from dark Rough-legs. Red-tails will hunt over any habitat, including city parks, but they are most numerous in farming country with some trees and woodlots. They are often seen perched in trees in fields or on fence posts along interstate highways.

[Ferruginous Hawk *(Buteo regalis)*]** *Hypothetical*. Only two reports exist of this western buteo, both by single observers: 24 November 1960, St. Louis Co.,and 20 January 1963, Wood River, Illinois. There are other reports, but the documentations fail to exclude the Krider's form of the Red-tailed Hawk.

Rough-legged Hawk *(Buteo lagopus)*. Although both light and dark color phases of this bird are found in the area, most observations are of light-phase individuals. It is often difficult to find during mild winters. When present, it inhabits open country alongside the Red-tail, which almost always outnumbers it.

Golden Eagle *(Aquila chrysaetos)*. Most reports of this western eagle in recent years have been from Busch CA, Carlyle Lake, and Mark Twain NWR.

American Kestrel *(Falco sparverius)*. The "grasslands" of the medians and shoulders of interstate highways provide hunting areas for the Kestrel, our most common falcon. It can be found hovering above its intended prey or perched conspicuously atop a tree or on a utility wire.

Merlin *(Falco columbarius)*. Most obser-vations of this scarce falcon are of brief "fly-bys" during migration. Although it is often seen near water, it can occur almost anywhere.

Merlin

Peregrine Falcon *(Falco peregrinus)*. The status of this large falcon is changing. The use of DDT almost caused its extermination, but the ban on the insecticide, coupled with reintroduction programs, is permitting it to make a comeback (or contributing to more sightings, at least). Birds seen outside of migration, particularly those seen in the city (St. Louis and Clayton), have probably been reintroduced locally. Migrants can occur almost anywhere but are most often found near shorebird or waterfowl concentrations.

Prairie Falcon *(Falco mexicanus)*. The majority of records have come from the lowlands of eastern St. Charles Co. and along the nearby bluffs bordering the Mississippi River west of Alton in Illinois. It has also been recorded from Busch CA, Carlyle Lake, and Calhoun Co.

GALLINACEOUS BIRDS

In addition to the five species discussed next, birders sometimes encounter other chicken-like birds. Chukar, California Quail, Guinea Fowl, and Peacock have each been observed in unexpected places. Such birds are either escaped domestic birds or birds introduced locally for hunting.

Ring-necked Pheasant *(Phasianus colchicus)* **Introduced.** Pheasants are established at Carlyle Lake, Mark Twain NWR, and in some areas of St. Charles Co., although their year to year abundance is variable. They can be found at Riverlands EDA, where they forage in the open fields at dusk and where the tall grass provides adequate cover for both roosting and breeding. They are not found in the southern part of our area, although suitable habitat appears to exist.

Ruffed Grouse *(Bonasa umbellus)* **Extirpated/Reintroduced.** In the early 1980's this grouse was reintroduced into areas where it was formerly a permanent resident. It can now be found rarely in Ste. Genevieve and Warren Cos., and there have been sightings from Busch CA and west St. Louis Co.

Greater Prairie-Chicken *(Tympanuchus cupido)* **Extirpated.** Common in the mid-1880's when there was still prairie habitat to support them, Prairie Chickens had decreased substantially in numbers by 1906, when there was still a month-long hunting season. The last known local flock was near O'Fallon, Illinois, in the early 1940's. Now they are found only in western Missouri (e.g., Barton and Dade Counties) and in central Illinois (Marion and Jasper Counties).

Wild Turkey *(Meleagris gallopavo)* **Extirpated/Reintroduced.** Introduced to replace a population that had almost become extirpated in the St. Louis area, turkeys have thrived to the extent that hunting was permitted by 1970 in three southern Illinois counties and by 1984 throughout Missouri. They are easiest to find in the Ozarks; locally, flocks of 10-100 birds can be seen in late fall and winter at Busch CA, Tyson Research Center, and Shaw Arboretum.

Northern Bobwhite *(Colinus virginianus).* Bobwhite occur in areas with fields separated by hedgerows and are most common where agriculture is not intense. Severe winters with prolonged snow and ice cover can reduce the Bobwhite's population. It is commonly found at Busch CA, Riverlands EDA, around Horseshoe and Carlyle Lakes, and in agricultural regions of Monroe and St. Clair Cos.

RAILS, GALLINULES, COOT, AND CRANES

Yellow Rail *(Coturnicops noveboracensis)*. This secretive little rail may be more common than the few records indicate. Wet meadows and grassy marshes are its favorite habitats. It has been found at Busch CA, Marais Temps Clair, and near Horseshoe Lake.

Black Rail *(Laterallus jamaicensis)*. Widmann (1907) mentions a bird of this species "taken once" in St. Charles Co., but gives no date or location. There is one other record: 15 August 1952 by a single observer at Marais Temps Clair.

King Rail *(Rallus elegans)*. This rail seems to be declining in numbers. With persistence it can be found in late spring and early summer at Marais Temps Clair, where it breeds.

Virginia Rail *(Rallus limicola)*. The Virginia Rail can sometimes be flushed by wading through marshes, but it is most often seen lurking at the edges of marshes or wet fields. It is an occasional breeder, if water conditions are favorable. Seek it at Marais Temps Clair, Riverlands EDA, and Horseshoe Lake.

Sora *(Porzana carolina)*. Our most common rail can be heard calling from marshes or damp meadows during migration. Like other rails, it is sometimes seen at vegetated edges of mudflats. Marais Temps Clair is the best place to find it.

Purple Gallinule *(Porphyrula martinica)*. There are ten records of this species for the St. Louis area. Two are from the 19th century, 18 April 1884 (St. Louis) and 22 April 1884 (St. Charles). Two others are of birds found dead: 1937 (St. Charles) and 1941 (Alton), exact dates unknown. The only recent fall record is a bird found injured in October 1951 (St. Charles Co., exact date unknown). Recent spring records range from 5 May to 8 June, with the most recent bird seen 5-13 May 1984 in a marsh along Illinois Hwy. 143, near the Alton power plant.

Common Moorhen *(Gallinula chloropus)*. This gallinule is a regular breeder at Horseshoe Lake, including the Eagle Park marsh area. It has also been found at Moredock Lake, Stump Lake, Riverlands EDA (Teal Pond), and Marais Temps Clair.

American Coot *(Fulica americana)*. Coots are numerous during migration, occurring in large raft-like flocks that seem to swarm over the water and adjacent shore. In mild winters they remain in our area. They are regular breeders at Eagle Park marsh, Marais Temps Clair, and Riverlands EDA.

Sandhill Crane *(Grus canadensis)*. There are only eleven records of Sandhill Crane for our area. St. Louis lies between the migration route that passes through the Great Plains to Texas and the route between the northern Midwest and the east coast. Most of our area records are of single individuals, sometimes in flocks of migrating geese. A flock of 30 on 14 April 1972 is the highest number recorded for the area.

Whooping Crane *(Grus americana) Extirpated.* Twelve of these cranes were seen flying over St. Louis on 25 March 1888. The last record for eastern Missouri was an immature seen by many observers at Mingo NWR between 30 November and 15 December 1958. An adult was seen and photographed near Hull, Pike Co., Illinois, between 16 October and 5 November 1958. Both of these 1958 records were outside the St. Louis area.

SHOREBIRDS

Of the 36 species of shorebirds that occur in our area, most are pass-through migrants; only four have bred in recent times (Killdeer, Spotted Sandpiper, Upland Sandpiper, and American Woodcock), and only the Killdeer is consistently found breeding. Shorebird abundance varies considerably from year to year because available habitat varies with seasonal rainfall and river conditions.

Black-bellied Plover *(Pluvialis squatarola)*. This plover is found on sandy beaches, flooded fields, or mudflats. Favorite locations are Horseshoe Lake and Riverlands EDA. In fall, juvenile birds resemble juvenile American Golden-Plovers, and the two species can be difficult to separate until they are seen in flight. The Black-bellied usually occurs in numbers from one to twelve.

American Golden-Plover *(Pluvialis dominica)*. Although it sometimes occurs on shorelines and mudflats, the American Golden-Plover is most often found on plowed or grassy fields, such as at St. Charles Airport. In spring, it can be seen in flocks of up to several hundred birds. Early first-year migrants in worn plumage can somewhat resemble Mountain Plovers.

Semipalmated Plover *(Charadrius semipalmatus)*. This species is usually found singly or in small flocks on mudflats, shorelines, and flooded fields, where it is sometimes seen running into bordering grass. A high count of 70 was observed 10 May 1986.

Piping Plover *(Charadrius melodus)*. Breeding populations of this small plover to our north have declined, so it has become an increasingly rare migrant here. Now seldom recorded, it can occur anywhere there are shorebirds. Most records are from Mueller Road lagoon, Riverlands EDA, and Horseshoe Lake.

Semipalmated Plover

Killdeer *(Charadrius vociferus)*. This plover is one of the most common and most universally distributed of the shorebirds in our area. Its preferred habitat varies from dry open fields to mudflats. It can be found nesting along gravel roads and sometimes on gravel rooftops. Its presence is usually revealed by its distinctive call.

Black-necked Stilt *(Himantopus mexicanus)*. There are six records of this southern shorebird: one, 3-4 May 1952 (near Taussig, St. Louis Co.); one, 21 August to 3 September 1969 (Madison Co.); one, 23 August to 28 September 1969 (St. Charles Co.); two, 30 June 1991 (Riverlands EDA); one or two, 17-27 June 1993 (Riverlands EDA); and a pair, 8-16 July 1993 (Fountain Creek, Monroe Co.) that were possibly breeders. The breeding range may be expanding northward, as a few nested in southeast Missouri in 1990.

American Avocet *(Recurvirostra americana)*. The avocet is found in flooded fields or mudflats. It is usually seen singly or in small flocks in this area; however, one flock of 47 was found on 22 April 1987 (Little Creve Coeur Lake).

Greater Yellowlegs *(Tringa melanoleuca)*. This species is found on mudflats, shorelines, and flooded fields, often feeding in shallow water. It is often found singly, but sometimes in small flocks.

Lesser Yellowlegs *(Tringa flavipes)*. The Lesser Yellowlegs occurs in the same habitat as the Greater, but often in larger flocks. It is one of the commonest and most readily observed of our migrant shorebirds.

Solitary Sandpiper *(Tringa solitaria)*. Look for this shorebird along edges of streams, ponds, and woodland pools, or on grassy mudflats. It occurs singly or in pairs and does not flock with other shorebirds.

Willet *(Catoptrophorus semipalmatus)*. This large shorebird is found in flooded fields, mudflats, and marshes. It is usually found singly, but a flock of 33 birds occurred on 4 May 1991 at Marais Temps Clair.

Spotted Sandpiper *(Actitis macularia)*. Like the Solitary, this sandpiper is almost always found singly or in pairs. In migration it prefers habitat like the Solitary's and can be found at Horseshoe Lake and Riverlands EDA. It has bred on island sandbars in area rivers and along shorelines of lakes and ponds.

Upland Sandpiper *(Bartramia longicauda)*. This species is a resident of grassy fields and prairies. It has bred locally, although there is presently little favorable habitat in our area. Almost all recent reports have been from the short-grass runways of St. Charles Airport.

Eskimo Curlew *(Numenius borealis) **Extirpated**. Formerly a common transient through Missouri, this species is on the verge of extinction. A specimen in the Hurter collection remains the only record; it was taken 10 April 1871 in St. Louis Co.

Whimbrel *(Numenius phaeopus)*. There are six records of this large shorebird for our area. The only fall record is of a single bird found on a sandbar in the Missouri River (St. Louis Co.) on 4 September 1949. The first four spring records are all of single birds: 25 May 1936 and 3 June 1954 (St. Charles Co.) and 23 May 1964 and 24 May 1969 (Monroe Co.). On 26 May 1983, two birds were found south of Fountain in Monroe Co.

Long-billed Curlew *(Numenius americanus) **Extirpated**. A specimen without data in the Hurter collection is the only record. Widmann (1907) states that the species formerly migrated through the Mississippi River valley, but he does not list any specific records. There is a possibility of recurrence; one was seen just north of our area on 2 April 1985 (Bohlen and Zimmerman, 1989).

Hudsonian Godwit *(Limosa haemastica)*. This godwit, found on mudflats and flooded fields with other shorebirds, is a sparse migrant here, since St. Louis lies east of its main spring migration corridor. Some observations have been of single birds, but flocks of up to 18 have occurred. There are three fall records: 6 October 1978 (Horseshoe Lake), 19-20 September 1979 (Horseshoe Lake), and 12 September 1982 (Hawthorne Street).

Marbled Godwit *(Limosa fedoa)*. In this area the Marbled Godwit is found on mudflats and flooded fields. All records have been of single birds, except for one flock of 17 on 27 April 1991 (Riverlands EDA).

Ruddy Turnstone *(Arenaria interpres)*. The Turnstone is usually reported from sandy beaches or mudflats. It has been found in many locations, but most recent records are from Chain of Rocks, Riverlands EDA, Horseshoe Lake, and Mueller Road lagoon. It occurs in numbers up to about twelve.

Red Knot *(Calidris canutus)*. The Red Knot prefers mudflats and sandy beaches. Most fall migrants are juvenile birds. There is only one spring record, 25 May 1950 (St. Louis Co.), and two late fall records, 10 November 1979 (Swan Lake) and 6 November 1981 (Alton dam).

Sanderling *(Calidris alba)*. As the name suggests, the Sanderling prefers sandy beaches, but it is also found on mudflats. It is most often found at Chain of Rocks but has also been seen at Horseshoe Lake, Mueller Road lagoon, and Riverlands EDA. It occurs singly or in small flocks. Two late migrants were seen at Riverlands EDA, 5-19 November 1992.

Semipalmated Sandpiper *(Calidris pusilla)*. This common "peep" is usually found on mudflats with other sandpipers. It tends to occur in smaller numbers than the Least, although a high count of 500 was found near the entrance to the Harbor Point (St. Charles Co.) on 18 May 1986.

Western Sandpiper *(Calidris mauri)*. The Western Sandpiper resembles the Semipalmated and is often found in the same locations, but it usually feeds in shallow water while the Semipalmated remains on the muddy edge. High counts range up to 60. For separation from the Semipalmated, see Kaufman (1990).

Western Sandpiper

Least Sandpiper *(Calidris minutilla)*. The Least is the most universally distributed of the "peep" sandpipers since it is found in flooded fields, grassy fields, and shorelines, as well as mudflats. It is also one of our most numerous shorebirds, sometimes occurring in flocks of hundreds in favorable habitat.

White-rumped Sandpiper *(Calidris fuscicollis)*. Look for this sandpiper in shallow water adjacent to mudflats, in flooded fields, and along shorelines. Few of this species have been recorded in fall because its main migration route is along the East Coast, but in spring it can be numerous toward the end of the shorebird migration period.

Baird's Sandpiper *(Calidris bairdii)*. This species is found on mudflats feeding near grassy borders, as well as on flooded or grassy fields and sandy beaches. It is most often seen in fall, individually or in small groups; virtually all of these fall birds are juveniles.

Pectoral Sandpiper *(Calidris melanotos)*. Mudflats, shorelines, flooded fields, and wet pastures are the preferred habitat of the Pectoral Sandpiper, one of our most abundant migrant shorebirds. Its numbers may exceed 1000 at peak times in good habitat.

[Purple Sandpiper *(Calidris maritima)*] *Hypothetical.* There is one report of this eastern shorebird for our area, a single bird near Orchard Farm (St. Charles Co.) on 4 May 1938. The species occasionally occurs in other parts of the midwest, so it might reasonably be seen here again. Its preferred habitat, rocky coasts, occurs along the large rivers (e.g., wing dams) and at Baldwin and Carlyle Lakes, but these areas are not routinely checked by observers.

Dunlin *(Calidris alpina)*. Dunlins are found on mudflats, shorelines, and flooded fields. The species is frequently reported from Swan Lake, Horseshoe Lake, Riverlands EDA, Mueller Road lagoon, Hawthorne Street, and Hayford Road.

Stilt Sandpiper *(Calidris himantopus)*. Stilt Sandpipers are found probing in shallow water, much like (and sometimes with) dowitchers. The spring flight is primarily west of our area, but in fall the species can be fairly numerous. A flock of 200 was reported on 29 August 1979 (Horseshoe Lake).

Buff-breasted Sandpiper *(Tryngites subruficollis)*. On mudflats and flooded fields, the Buff-breasted Sandpiper is usually found away from the water, near grassy borders. It is also found in short-grass fields such as those found at airports, parks, and sod farms. It has been seen at Chain of Rocks, Horseshoe Lake, and Eagle Park. A high count of 50 occurred on 6 September 1970 (St. Charles Co.). There are only three spring records, all of single birds: 9 April 1967, 25 May 1985, and 7 May 1987.

Ruff *(Philomachus pugnax)*. Two birds at Busch CA on 7 October 1962 established the first area record. Since then there have been eight more sightings, three of which were in spring: 8 May 1981 (Horseshoe Lake), 19 May 1984 (Monroe Co.), and 24 April 1988 (Mark Twain NWR).

Short-billed Dowitcher *(Limnodromus griseus)*.
Long-billed Dowitcher *(Limnodromus scolopaceus)*. Both dowitchers probe the mud in shallow water of mudflats and flooded fields and occur in small flocks of up to 20. The two dowitchers strongly resemble each other and are difficult to distinguish, except in juvenal plumage; further-more, some reports may have been based on misleading criteria in some field guides. Because of these problems, the **SEASONAL OCCURRENCE** bar graphs for these two species (based on reported observations) may be inaccurate. Short-bills probably predominate numerically when they are here, but (based on data for other areas) Long-bills occur earlier in spring and later in fall. Short-billed Dowitchers that migrate through St. Louis are the *hendersoni* race. The most reliable means of distinguishing the two species is by call note. For identification see Hayman et al. (1986) and Kaufman (1990).

Common Snipe *(Gallinago gallinago)*. Snipe are found in marshes, swamps, wet fields, mudflats, and roadside ditches. They usually occur individually or in small numbers. Look for them at Eagle Park marsh, Hayford Road, Riverlands EDA, Swan Lake, and Marais Temps Clair. Some snipe will winter here if conditions are mild, and an occasional bird may be found along flowing water.

American Woodcock *(Scolopax minor)*. This unique shorebird feeds in wet woodlands but is usually observed during breeding season as it dis-plays at dusk or dawn in open areas bordering woods. Look for it in early spring at Busch CA or Weldon Spring CA, where it is known to breed.

Wilson's Phalarope *(Phalaropus tricolor)*. The Wilson's, the only phalarope to occur in our area annually, is usually found in the shallow water of flooded fields or mudflats. Swan Lake, Horseshoe Lake, and Riverlands EDA are places to find it if water levels are right.

Red-necked Phalarope *(Phalaropus lobatus)*. Look for this scarce phalarope in flooded fields, sewage lagoons, mudflats, and near lake shores. Most reports are from Horseshoe Lake and the Mueller Road lagoon, where it is usually seen swimming, rather than feeding on the mud.

Red Phalarope *(Phalaropus fulicaria)*. This rare phalarope is found in the same habitat as the other two phalaropes. Horseshoe Lake, Carlyle Lake, and Busch CA have provided six of the eleven records. There is one summer record of 28-29 July 1974 (St. Charles Co.) and a winter record of 6-12 January 1992 (Carlyle Lake).

Pomarine Jaeger *(Stercorarius pomarinus)*. This jaeger is attracted by large concentrations of gulls along rivers or large lakes. Most sightings are in late fall, but there is one summer record of 9-12 July 1981 (Alton dam) and a winter record of 27 February 1991 (Riverlands EDA). Carlyle Lake and the Riverlands EDA/Alton area provide the most sightings.

Pomarine Jaeger

Parasitic Jaeger
(Stercorarius parasiticus).
There are three accepted records: 10-17 November 1985 at Carlyle Lake, 6 October 1988 at Carlyle Lake, and 2 November 1991 at Riverlands EDA.

GULLS

Perhaps no other family of birds has so drastically increased in numbers in recent years as have the gulls. Until 1950, only four species of gull had been recorded for the St. Louis area; as of 1994, the list was up to eighteen. For the common gulls, the numbers of individuals have also increased dramatically.

Laughing Gull *(Larus atricilla)*. First discovered at the Alton dam on 30 May 1955, this gull is becoming more regular each year. Most reports are from the large rivers and lakes, but it has also been reported from flooded fields. Birds in the distinctive juvenal plumage have occurred in the late summer and fall.

Franklin's Gull *(Larus pipixcan)*. This gull, a migrant to and from its prairie breeding grounds, is most commonly found in fall at Swan Lake or Carlyle Lake, where as many as 100 have been seen in one day. In second-year plumage it can sometimes be confused with the Laughing Gull; see Kaufman (1990).

Little Gull *(Larus minutus)*. The Little Gull was first discovered in our area on 14 November 1962 (Holten State Park). In total, there have been twelve records of the species, but only three in spring: 18 and 24 April 1984 (Carlyle Lake; probably the same bird) and 4 April 1991 (Riverlands EDA).

Common Black-headed Gull *(Larus ridibundus)*. This European gull has occurred twice: 4 December 1985 to 4 January 1986 (Horseshoe Lake) and 10-25 September 1988 (below the old Alton dam at the present location of Riverlands EDA).

Bonaparte's Gull *(Larus philadelphia)*. This species, our smallest regular gull, is found on rivers, lakes, mudflats, and sewage lagoons in small flocks. Most winter reports are from the artificially warmed waters of Baldwin Lake. There is one early-fall record of 11 August 1991 (Riverlands EDA).

Mew Gull *(Larus canus)*. The only accepted record of this western species in the St. Louis area is that of a single adult bird seen by many observers between 12 February and 8 March 1986 at Carlyle Lake.

Ring-billed Gull *(Larus delawarensis)*.
Herring Gull *(Larus argentatus)*. Inasmuch as these two common gulls overlap in distribution and abundance, they are discussed together here. The SEASONAL OCCURRENCE bar graphs fail to indicate the variability in abundance depending on the severity of the winter. In the fall, immature Ring-bills are the first to arrive in our area, followed by Ring-billed Gull adults and Herring Gull immatures, and finally by Herring Gull adults. Many of the immature Ring-bills continue farther south. If the winter is

mild, the distribution is about 100 Ring-bills for every Herring. However, if the winter becomes severe, the Ring-billed Gulls move farther south, more Herring Gulls arrive from the north, and the abundance ratio reverses. This is a simplified description of the gulls' movements; in reality there is much overlap as abundance patterns shift with the weather. When winter moderates, the adult Herring Gulls are the first to leave and Ring-billed Gulls return, especially immatures. As many as 10,000 gulls of either species can winter in our area. Small numbers of Ring-bills linger along the Mississippi River through midsummer, when Herring Gulls are absent, although there is an early fall record of a year-old Herring Gull on 11 August 1991 (Riverlands EDA).

California Gull *(Larus californicus)*. This western species was first reported on 5 April 1975 at the Alton dam and has been found subsequently on ten occasions. Great care should be taken with identification of subadult birds.

Thayer's Gull *(Larus thayeri)*. First identified on 11 October 1975 at the Alton dam, this gull has since become an annual visitor. It is most numerous during severe winters when several may sometimes be found in a day. Most records come from the Mississippi River. Identification is covered in detail in Kaufman (1990).

Iceland Gull *(Larus glaucoides)*. This gull was first found on 10 February 1957 at the Alton dam. Most of the 29 records are of single birds (*kumlieni* race) seen in the Alton area of the Mississippi River; it is most commonly seen in severe winters. Some of the early records may actually have been Thayer's or Glaucous Gulls.

Lesser Black-backed Gull *(Larus fuscus)*. Although it was only first recorded on 30 December 1980 (Chain of Rocks), reports of this gull are increasingly frequent, with five sightings during the winter of 1992-93. Most birds have been reported from the Mississippi River and Carlyle Lake.

Slaty-backed Gull *(Larus schistisagus)*. Probably the most famous bird to visit St. Louis was a Slaty-backed Gull. An adult bird was seen along the Mississippi River from the Alton dam south to Mosenthein Island between 20 December 1983 and 29 January 1984. Many out-of-town observers came to see the bird because it was the first known occurrence of this Siberian/Alaskan species in the lower 48 United States.

Glaucous Gull *(Larus hyperboreus)*. This large gull was first discovered in our area on 29 December 1950 at the Alton dam. It is now seen almost every year, more commonly during severe winters. Most sightings have been from the Alton area of the Mississippi River. There is one late spring record of 26 May 1978 (St. Charles Co.) and an early fall record of 20 October 1991 (Carlyle Lake).

Great Black-backed Gull *(Larus marinus)*. An adult bird was found at the Alton dam on 15 February 1968 for the first area record. There have been 28 records since 1978, mostly from Carlyle Lake, Horseshoe Lake, and the Alton area of the Mississippi River.

Black-legged Kittiwake *(Rissa tridactyla)*. The first occurrence of this species was at the Alton dam on 29 January 1967. Twenty-four birds, almost all singles in first-winter plumage, have been recorded in our area, mostly from Carlyle and Horseshoe Lakes and along the Mississippi River.

Ross's Gull *(Rhodostethia rosea)*. This arctic species has occurred once, an adult discovered at Riverlands EDA on 31 December 1991 that obligingly stayed until 9 January 1992. This ten-day stay allowed many out-of-state birders to see the rare bird, which was the subject of countless photographs and videos.

Sabine's Gull *(Xema sabini)*. The Alton dam provided the first area record of this species on 12 September 1965. Although it has been seen at Swan Lake, Horseshoe Lake, and the Alton dam, six of the ten records have been from Carlyle Lake, where a high of seven individuals was seen during the period of 23-28 September 1986.

Common Tern

TERNS

Caspian Tern *(Sterna caspia)*. Formerly, this large tern was usually seen singly, but small flocks are now common. Look for it on large rivers and lakes.

Common Tern *(Sterna hirundo)*. The Common Tern and the Forster's Tern are difficult to distinguish in some plumages. Despite its name, this tern is usually the less common of the two in our area. Both species can be found on rivers, lakes, or marshes.

Forster's Tern *(Sterna forsteri)*. See Common Tern. The Forster's is a regular and easily observed migrant. There is one late winter record: 10 February 1991 (Portage Des Sioux).

Least Tern *(Sterna antillarum)*. The Least Tern nested locally on sandbars in the Mississippi River as late as the 1970's, and it still nests south of our area. The species is endangered over much of its range, and only one or two sightings are now made in our area each year. Horseshoe and Baldwin Lakes and Riverlands EDA have provided most of the recent records.

Black Tern *(Chlidonias niger)*. This species formerly bred in our area when a greater amount of marshland existed. It migrates in small loose flocks along rivers and between lakes, feeding primarily on insects.

DOVES, PARROTS, AND CUCKOOS

Rock Dove *(Columba livia)*. *Introduced.* "Pigeons" are most easily found under bridges and overpasses, in city parks, and on grain barges in the rivers, although some still nest in more "natural" habitat like quarries. Many color and pattern variations occur and some individuals can be confusing when they occur out of context.

[Ringed Turtle-Dove *(Streptopelia risoria)*] *Introduced/Not Established.* This dove is occasionally seen in Tower Grove Park and elsewhere in the metropolitan part of the area. Most sightings are believed to be of escaped cage birds.

Mourning Dove *(Zenaida macroura)*. This adaptable dove is equally at home in urban and rural settings. It is commonly found at feeders and grain spills.

Passenger Pigeon *(Ectopistes migratorius)* *Extinct.* Although formerly one of the most abundant migrants through our area, St. Louis was south of its main breeding range. It was last reported from Missouri in Franklin Co. in September 1902 (Robbins and Easterla, 1992).

[Monk Parakeet *(Myiopsitta monachus)*] *Introduced/Not Established.* Some of these South American birds have evidently been released by pet owners and others may have simply escaped. Although individuals are occasionally seen in Tower Grove Park and in various rural regions, the species is not yet established in our area.

Carolina Parakeet *(Conuropsis carolinensis)* ***Extinct.*** This species was formerly common in forests along the large rivers; it was last seen in Illinois and Missouri in 1912 (Bohlen and Zimmerman, 1989; Robbins and Easterla, 1992).

Black-billed Cuckoo *(Coccyzus erythropthalmus)*. Both cuckoos prefer riparian habitat and woodland edges. They are sometimes seen flying across rural roads from one hedgerow to another. Although usually seen only during migration, the Black-billed Cuckoo may be a rare breeder in our area.

Yellow-billed Cuckoo *(Coccyzus americanus)*. During migration, this cuckoo can be found almost anywhere and is often spotted in places with migrant passerines. In the breeding season it is widespread in all forested areas, although it varies in abundance from year to year and is heard more often than seen.

OWLS

Barn Owl *(Tyto alba)*. Never common in our area, this owl has been a victim in part of modern farming practices and is seldom encountered now. Most recent sightings have been of birds released to reestablish the population. Any sightings of Barn Owls should be reported to either the Missouri or Illinois Departments of Conservation.

Eastern Screech-Owl *(Otus asio)*. Despite an abundance of apparently favorable habitat in our area, most reports of this species are from the suburbs, and parks like Forest Park and Tower Grove Park. Individuals usually return regularly to favorite roosting holes or nest boxes and are easy to see once they are discovered. Because they are so nocturnal, screech-owls are probably more common than generally thought.

Great Horned Owl *(Bubo virginianus)*. Also more common than generally recognized, this widespread owl is equally at home in parks, residential neighborhoods, and rural regions. During late evening and early morning twilight hours, it may sometimes be seen silhouetted against the sky on tree branches and utility poles.

Snowy Owl *(Nyctea scandiaca)*. There have been fewer than ten records for our area. Several of these birds have remained in the area for most of the winter; others have stayed only briefly.

Barred Owl *(Strix varia)*. This common resident of the bottomland forests is often heard to "hoot" during the day and sometimes responds to imitations of its call. It is most often seen in winter, when the trees are bare, or in late spring, when it has young to feed. Seek it at Busch CA, Mark Twain NWR, Weldon Spring CA, and Shaw Arboretum.

Long-eared Owl *(Asio otus)*. During the winter this owl is usually found roosting in pine trees, commonly in small groups. Although there have been no recent reports of breeding, it has nested at Rockwoods and Busch CA.

Short-eared Owl *(Asio flammeus)*. This is the least nocturnal of the owls that regularly occur in our area; sometimes several birds are seen hunting in the same field at dusk. In the early 1980's it was regularly found at St. Charles Co. Airport, but it is seldom seen there now because the grassy borders of the runways are more manicured. Most recent sightings have occurred at Marais Temps Clair, Riverlands EDA, and reclaimed strip mines in Illinois.

Northern Saw-whet Owl *(Aegolius acadicus)*. This nocturnal owl is only observed every few years, but it is probably more common than the few reports would indicate. Like the Screech Owl, it is often discovered first by small birds like chickadees; the mobbing racket that ensues then attracts humans. Whitewash and pellets on the ground under roosts in conifers and grapevine tangles also help reveal its presence. Saw-whets have been found in residential neighborhoods, Busch CA, and Hazlet State Park. Although breeding has not been confirmed, there is a specimen of a juvenile Saw-whet Owl found dead in a parking lot near Tower Grove Park.

NIGHTJARS, SWIFTS, AND HUMMINGBIRDS

Common Nighthawk *(Chordeiles minor)*. Although found in rural parts of our area, nighthawks are most often seen in the city where they nest on flat gravel roofs. They are most evident at dusk and early evening catching insects around the powerful lights of ballfields, shopping malls, and billboards. During the fall migration they are sometimes seen in large numbers at dusk.

Chuck-will's-widow *(Caprimulgus carolinensis)*. Most reports are from south of the city (Jefferson Co.), but the species is regularly reported from Busch CA and has occurred in suburban parks in migration.

Whip-poor-will *(Caprimulgus vociferus).* This nightjar is easy to hear, but hard to see. When breeding, they are most vocal just after sunset. During migration individuals can occasionally be flushed from low roosts or spotted while roosting lengthwise on limbs during daylight. On cool evenings Whip-poor-wills sometimes roost on warm asphalt roads in wooded regions, and can be seen by driving slowly and stopping when "eyeshine" from head lamps is reflected back.

Chimney Swift *(Chaetura pelagica).* These gregarious aerialists can be seen and heard almost constantly overhead in cities and suburbs in summer. They nest and roost in big chimneys, where they can be seen returning in large numbers at dusk, particularly in late summer.

Ruby-throated Hummingbird *(Archilochus colubris).* Although it breeds in our area, the Ruby-throat is often difficult to find when sought. It sometimes perches on wires along rural roads. The largest numbers are seen in fall, when immature migrants frequent feeders and fields of flowering weeds. Any late fall hummingbird (October and later) should be studied carefully, as most records for *Selasphorus* hummingbirds (Rufous and Allen's) for western Missouri and neighboring states have occurred at this time.

KINGFISHER AND WOODPECKERS

Belted Kingfisher *(Ceryle alcyon).*
Kingfishers are widespread along rivers, streams, and small bodies of water such as the lagoons in Forest Park. During the winter they may remain wherever there is open water and fish. Most Kingfisher sightings are preceded by the hearing of its rattle-like call. It occurs singly or in pairs.

juvenile Kingfisher

Red-headed Woodpecker
(Melanerpes erythrocephalus).
Although a year-round resident, this woodpecker also migrates through our area, and in April and May it may be encountered in small flocks (6 or less) in places where it is not usually seen. During the breeding season it is found in fields with scattered trees or on utility poles. In winter it is more

common some years than others, and is usually found in riverbottom forests. It may be decreasing in numbers.

Red-bellied Woodpecker *(Melanerpes carolinus)*. The Red-bellied is more common in suburban settings than the Red-headed and is a conspicuous resident of virtually all woodlands.

Yellow-bellied Sapsucker *(Sphyrapicus varius)*. Sapsuckers may appear in any place with trees; in winter look for them in groves of conifers. They are often seen in Tower Grove Park. This is the only woodpecker that occurs in our area that does not breed here, although it was a rare breeder in the 19th century.

Downy Woodpecker *(Picoides pubescens)*. The Downy, our smallest and most widespread woodpecker, can occur any place where trees grow, from forests to subdivisions. It is often seen at feeders, and occasionally on large weeds and cornstalks.

Hairy Woodpecker *(Picoides villosus)*. The Hairy is outnumbered by its smaller look-alike. It prefers mature woodlands but it is sometimes found in residential areas, especially in winter.

Northern Flicker *(Colaptes auratus)*. The Flicker, found in a wide range of habitats, is probably the most frequently seen woodpecker after the Downy. It often feeds on the ground and sometimes visits feeders. During the spring it has the noisy habit of hammering on drain pipes and street lamps. The western race ("Red-shafted") has been seen rarely in our area during the winter.

Pileated Woodpecker *(Dryocopus pileatus)*. This woodpecker is most easily found in extensive tracts of riverbottom woodlands. Because of fragmentation of such forests, it is less common now than formerly. It may be seen in suburban areas with large trees. Seek it at Castlewood State Park, Shaw Arboretum, Weldon Spring CA (Lewis and Clark Trails), and Mark Twain NWR.

Ivory-billed Woodpecker *(Campephilus principalis)* **Extirpated.** Formerly an uncommon resident along the Mississippi River, this species has not been seen in Missouri or Illinois since the 19th century (Robbins and Easterla, 1992; Bohlen and Zimmerman, 1989). A specimen exists in the Denver Museum of Natural History of a female collected near Forest Park on 8 May 1886.

FLYCATCHERS

Olive-sided Flycatcher *(Contopus borealis)*. This scarce migrant flycatcher is usually seen perched on the topmost branch of a dead tree. It occasionally gives its distinctive 3-note song in spring. Tower Grove Park is the best place to seek it.

Eastern Wood-Pewee *(Contopus virens)*. The Pewee, a forest bird, is the most common flycatcher of wooded areas in summer. It is often seen on a low branch calling out its name.

Yellow-bellied Flycatcher *(Empidonax flaviventris)*. The Yellow-bellied Flycatcher is best identified in spring when it occasionally calls. It often remains below eye level, and feeds in denser understory than other *Empidonax* flycatchers. Most reports are from Forest Park and Tower Grove Park.

Acadian Flycatcher *(Empidonax virescens)*. The Acadian is the only widespread breeding *Empidonax* flycatcher in our area. It nests along wooded streams and in bottomland forests, where its explosive song reveals its presence.

Alder Flycatcher *(Empidonax alnorum)*. This seldom-seen flycatcher is found only during migration, and usually occurs in higher and drier habitat than the following species, from which it can be separated best by song or call.

Willow Flycatcher *(Empidonax traillii)*. As its name implies, the Willow Flycatcher is usually found in willows near ponds, streams, and marshes. A localized breeding bird, not very numerous, it can usually be found at Marais Temps Clair, Chain of Rocks, and Busch CA.

Least Flycatcher *(Empidonax minimus)*. The Least is vociferous in spring and is usually the easiest *Empidonax* to find in migrant traps like Forest Park and Tower Grove Park. In 1992, a pair of Least Flycatchers attempted to breed just to the west of our area in Montgomery Co., for the first known breeding attempt in Missouri in nearly 100 years; there are also summer records for other parts of Missouri.

Eastern Phoebe *(Sayornis phoebe)*. The hardiest of the flycatchers, the Phoebe has sometimes been seen on Christmas Bird Counts. It is often found nesting under bridges and overhangs of rural buildings.

Say's Phoebe *(Sayornis saya)*. The only record for our area is an individual found 28 December 1952 at Busch CA.

Vermilion Flycatcher *(Pyrocephalus rubinus)*. There are three records of this species, all from Busch CA: an immature male, 11-23 November 1952; three females and an immature male, 30 September 1967 (the females were soon gone, but the male remained until found dead on 13 November); and another male, 28 September 1972.

Great Crested Flycatcher *(Myiarchus crinitus)*. This forest cavity nester is widespread and easily located by its call. It nests in Forest Park and Tower Grove Park as well as many rural woodlots.

Western Kingbird *(Tyrannus verticalis)*. A rare migrant, this western species has also been found nesting since 1984. It has bred regularly since 1986 on utility poles near Hall Street and East Grand Blvd. More recently it has been found at Second Street and Russell Blvd., with no evidence of breeding. Both of these locations are industrial areas of the city.

Eastern Kingbird *(Tyrannus tyrannus)*. Our common kingbird is widespread and is often seen flycatching from utility wires throughout our area. It occurs in city parks but it is more common outside the city.

Scissor-tailed Flycatcher *(Tyrannus forficatus)*. This species was first observed on the floodplain of Monroe Co. on 20 May 1967. Over the next 23 years there were about ten more records, usually of birds that did not linger long in our area. However, in 1991 a pair nested and raised four young on a utility pole near I-44 in west St. Louis Co. Although most sightings have been in May, there are fall records of 5 September 1982 and 26-27 October 1984, both from Belleville.

HORNED LARK AND SWALLOWS

Horned Lark *(Eremophila alpestris)*. This ground bird is a common breeder in fields of Illinois and eastern St. Charles Co., Missouri. Larks often feed in the gravel of roadsides, and in winter they sometimes gather in large flocks. A few individuals of the northern subspecies *E. a. alpestris* mingle with the local subspecies *E. a. praticola* in winter.

Purple Martin *(Progne subis).*
This large swallow is attracted to
martin houses in the city and suburbs (Forest Park, Missouri Botanical
Garden) and prefers a nearby source of
open water. It sometimes roosts in large
numbers in willows along rivers in late
August.

Purple Martin

Tree Swallow *(Tachycineta
bicolor).* This species is an
uncommon breeding swallow but
a very common migrant. Flocks
of thousands occur in fall, usually near open
water or perched on utility wires.

**Northern Rough-
winged Swallow**
*(Stelgidopteryx serripe-
nis).* Rough-wings nest
locally in banks,
bluffs, and roadside cuts.
They are com-
monly found
along our larger
streams and rivers in
summer. Like Tree Swallows, they form large flocks in fall.

Bank Swallow *(Riparia riparia).* The Bank Swallow breeds locally in
colonies in eroded riverbanks, quarries, and roadcuts, but few such
colonies occur in our area. It is more widespread and numerous in migration.

Cliff Swallow *(Hirundo pyrrhonota).* This species nests in colonies under
bridges or eaves of buildings. Like the Bank Swallow, nesting colonies are
rare in our area and often are abandoned after a few years, but the species
is seen frequently as a migrant.

Barn Swallow *(Hirundo rustica).* Found throughout the countryside, the
Barn Swallow is our most common breeding swallow. It commonly nests

in eaves of barns, but also in untraditional locations like parking ramps at shopping malls.

JAYS AND CROWS

Blue Jay *(Cyanocitta cristata)*. No species better typifies the Missouri Ozarks area than the Blue Jay. It is a common suburban species but difficult to find in agricultural regions of Illinois. The species is migratory, and loose flocks of hundreds are sometimes seen in fall.

[Black-billed Magpie *(Pica pica)*] *Hypothetical.* There is one report of this species, 17 January 1975 at Busch CA. The bird may have escaped captivity.

American Crow *(Corvus brachyrhynchos)*. Crows are abundant, both in the suburbs and the countryside. In winter, large numbers can be seen flying to roost sites at dusk.

Fish Crow *(Corvus ossifragus)*. This small crow was first observed in the levee region of Monroe Co. in August, 1962. Now the range has expanded, and it has been found along large rivers throughout our area. Breeding was finally confirmed in 1990 and 1991 at Gilbert Lake.

CHICKADEES, TITMOUSE, NUTHATCHES, AND CREEPER

Black-capped Chickadee *(Parus atricapillus)*.
Carolina Chickadee *(Parus carolinensis)*. The boundary between the ranges of these two chickadees passes through the St. Louis area. Black-capped Chickadees can be found as far south as Edwardsville, west through Jersey and Calhoun Counties in Illinois and southwest through northern St. Charles Co. to Busch CA in Missouri. Carolina Chickadees range north to Carlyle and Horseshoe Lakes in Illinois, and west through St. Louis Co. into Franklin Co. in Missouri. The area between the two ranges is a contact zone. This zone is approximately between Edwardsville and Horseshoe Lake, west through north St. Louis Co.,

Carolina Chickadees

the city of St. Louis, southwest St. Louis Co., and along the Missouri River in south St. Charles and Franklin Cos. Chickadees in the contact zone usually resemble Carolinas in appearance, but sing atypical three-note (sometimes four- or five-note) songs. Most of these birds are probably hybrids. Thus, chickadees in the contact zone cannot always be identified as to species. There are erratic southward movements of Black-capped Chickadees during the winter.

Tufted Titmouse *(Parus bicolor).* This resident species is found throughout our area in a variety of wooded habitats, often in small groups or families. It is a common feeder visitor.

Red-breasted Nuthatch *(Sitta canadensis).* This nuthatch is an erratic visitor from the north. Some years it is not reported at all, most years only a few individuals are seen, but some years major flights occur. Early fall sightings may forecast major invasion years. During late fall and winter they are found most regularly in conifers at Busch CA and Shaw Arboretum, and sometimes at feeders.

White-breasted Nuthatch *(Sitta carolinensis).* The White-breasted is the resident nuthatch of our area and can be found in any place with numerous large trees. It often visits feeders in winter.

White-breasted Nuthatch

Brown-headed Nuthatch *(Sitta pusilla) Extirpated.* There is one record of this species for our area, from a private park in south St. Louis on 6 May 1878.

Brown Creeper *(Certhia americana).* The creeper occurs in any area with deciduous trees and is often detected by its high, thin call note. Although more common as a migrant, it can also be found in small numbers in winter, moving through the woods with chickadees, titmice, and nuthatches. There have been no local breeding records since 1909.

WRENS

Rock Wren *(Salpinctes obsoletus)*. There have been two sightings of this western species: 11-19 October 1978 (Horseshoe Lake) and 10-15 November 1990 (Carlyle Lake).

Carolina Wren *(Thryothorus ludovicianus)*. This wren is found throughout our area in wooded habitat and suburbs. Its numbers were greatly reduced after several severe winters in the late 1970's, but it gradually recovered during the following milder winters. It sings year round and visits feeders in winter.

Bewick's Wren *(Thryomanes bewickii)*. Never common, this wren is probably decreasing in numbers. An early migrant and breeder, it is usually found in rural Jefferson and Franklin Cos. in brushpiles, fencerows, and yards.

House Wren *(Troglodytes aedon)*. The House Wren is the common wren of the city, suburbs, farmyards, and woodlots, where its constant exuberant song can be heard throughout the nesting season.

Winter Wren *(Troglodytes troglodytes)*. Seek this wren in brush piles and fallen logs near wooded streams and in riverbottoms. It is most often seen at Tower Grove Park, Forest Park, and Busch CA.

Sedge Wren *(Cistothorus platensis)*. This wren is found in fields of dense grass or weeds during migration. It has bred in late July and early August at Marais Temps Clair,

Sedge Wren

Riverlands EDA, Mark Twain NWR, and Gordon Moore Park in Alton, although suitable habitat is not available every year. There have been two early winter records from Pere Marquette State Park on Christmas Bird Counts, 21 December 1968 and 26 December 1971. It is best found by its frequent song.

Marsh Wren *(Cistothorus palustris)*. The Marsh Wren is found in places with extensive cattail marsh, such as Marais Temps Clair, Horseshoe Lake, and Riverlands EDA, where its distinctive song reveals its presence. During migration it can be found among roots of trees at the water's edge or sometimes in wet grassy fields. It probably breeds in our area.

KINGLETS AND GNATCATCHER

Golden-crowned Kinglet *(Regulus satrapa)*. As a winter visitor that favors conifers, this little bird spends most of its time in the tree tops in small flocks and is not often seen. It also migrates through wooded areas and suburbs. Once one is attuned to its high-pitched, three-note call, it is easy to locate.

Ruby-crowned Kinglet *(Regulus calendula)*. This kinglet migrates with the warblers and is sometimes mistaken for one. It is one of the most numerous migrant passerines, and occasionally remains in the area through the winter.

Blue-gray Gnatcatcher *(Polioptila caerulea)*. This species breeds in deciduous forests and is usually easy to locate by its persistent call.

THRUSHES

Eastern Bluebird *(Sialia sialis)*. The state bird of Missouri is producing more young as a result of an increased number of nest boxes (Robbins and Easterla, 1992). It prefers open fields or golf courses with scattered trees and other perches adjacent to woodlands. It is often seen perched on fence and utility wires in rural regions such as Shaw Arboretum and Busch CA.

Veery *(Catharus fuscescens)*. The Veery is the least common of the migrant thrushes in our area. Like the other *Catharus* thrushes, it is usually seen feeding on the ground. Tower Grove Park is the premier place to observe all the migrant thrushes in spring.

Gray-cheeked Thrush *(Catharus minimus)*. The Gray-cheek is more common than the Veery but less common than the Swainson's Thrush. Like the Veery, it sometimes calls but does not sing as frequently as the Swainson's while migrating through our area.

Swainson's Thrush *(Catharus ustulatus)*. It is common to find 20 or more individuals in Forest Park or Tower Grove Park at the peak of spring migration. This thrush can also be heard singing and calling in suburban neighborhoods in May.

Hermit Thrush *(Catharus guttatus)*. The Hermit is the only *Catharus* thrush to occasionally winter in our area, where it is found in riverbottoms, pine groves, and cedars. It rarely sings during its stay in the St. Louis area.

Swainson's Thrush

Wood Thrush *(Hylocichla mustelina)*. Although not as common now as formerly, the Wood Thrush is the only spotted thrush to breed in our area. It is found in bottomland forests and lower elevations and is most vocal early in the morning and at dusk.

American Robin *(Turdus migratorius)*. Robins seem to prefer the suburbs during the breeding season, but they occur in surprisingly large flocks in riverbottoms and open country with cedar trees in winter. During the winter of 1964-1965 a roost of some three million birds was studied in Jefferson Co.

Varied Thrush *(Ixoreus naevius)*. The only area record is a single bird seen 18-26 December 1976 (Calhoun Co.). This is the southernmost record for Illinois.

CATBIRD, MOCKINGBIRD, AND THRASHER

Gray Catbird *(Dumetella carolinensis)*. This mimic is found throughout our area in places with dense shrubbery or understory. It usually stays below eye level.

Northern Mockingbird *(Mimus polyglottos)*. This conspicuous resident is found throughout the area but is most abundant in the suburbs. In winter, the local population consists largely of males. The curse of insomniacs, mockingbirds sometimes sing throughout the night.

Brown Thrasher *(Toxostoma rufum).* Our only thrasher is occasionally seen in winter around feeders. During the summer it is easily found in hedgerows and along wooded edges throughout our area.

PIPITS, WAXWINGS, SHRIKES, AND STARLING

American Pipit *(Anthus rubescens).* The abundance of this ground-feeding species depends on the availability of wet or flooded fields, where it is most often found in small flocks. The most reliable locations have been Riverlands EDA, Mark Twain NWR, and Busch CA.

Sprague's Pipit *(Anthus spragueii).* There is one accepted record of two individuals seen by a single observer on 19 October 1992 at the St. Charles Airport. Earlier reports from as late as 1952 are suspect because of the difficulty in identification.

Bohemian Waxwing *(Bombycilla garrulus).* Outside of an invasion in 1962, there have been few records of this erratic northern species; these sightings have involved only one or two birds each, mostly from Busch CA. There have been no more than five records since 1962.

Cedar Waxwing *(Bombycilla cedrorum).* Our common waxwing is usually seen in flocks. Some years it is more abundant than others. Its abundance in winter depends on the availability of cedar, poison ivy, and other small berries.

[Northern Shrike *(Lanius excubitor)*] *Hypothetical.* Seldom observed as far south as St. Louis, the last report of this species was on 19 February 1950 (St. Charles Co.).

Loggerhead Shrike *(Lanius ludovicianus).* Less common on the Missouri side of the Mississippi River, this species prefers the open spaces of the Illinois prairie. Numbers have declined over the past 30 years.

European Starling *(Sturnus vulgaris)* **Introduced.** The Starling was introduced in New York in 1890-91 and reached St. Louis in 1929. It roosts in large flocks in many locations.

VIREOS

White-eyed Vireo *(Vireo griseus)*. This
vireo occurs throughout our area
in second-growth edge, brambles,
thickets, and grapevine tangles,
where its distinctive song reveals
its presence. It is common at Busch
CA.

White-eyed Vireo

Bell's Vireo *(Vireo bellii)*.
Both the White-eyed and
Bell's are usually found
closer to the ground than the other vireos, but the Bell's prefers more open
habitat, such as hedgerows, and is more local in its distribution. Although
it is difficult to see, it can be located by its repetitive song. It is regularly
found at Busch CA.

Solitary Vireo *(Vireo solitarius)*. During the spring migration, the
Solitary Vireo is usually located by its song. It is often easier to find in fall
when it lingers in our area longer.

Yellow-throated Vireo *(Vireo flavifrons)*. This colorful vireo breeds
locally in mature forests and river bottoms and is occasionally found in
trees in open areas.

Warbling Vireo *(Vireo gilvus)*. Look for this species in cottonwoods
along rivers, streams, and ponds such as the lagoons in Forest Park. It
usually feeds high in trees, making it difficult to see, but it is common and
readily located by its song.

Philadelphia Vireo *(Vireo philadelphicus)*. This vireo is regularly found
in Forest Park and Tower Grove Park during migration. Its song is easily
confused with that of the Red-eyed Vireo.

Red-eyed Vireo *(Vireo olivaceus)*. This is the most common breeding
vireo of large woodland tracts. Like other vireos, it sings incessantly during breeding season, even in the afternoon when most other songbirds are
silent.

WARBLERS

Of the 38 species of warblers that have occurred in the St. Louis area, 36 are seen almost every year and 17 breed locally. Nearly all of the others breed farther north and pass through our area in spring and fall. Warblers are most easily identified in spring by their bright plumages and songs. Although they occur almost anywhere in migration and are often seen and heard in residential areas, most birders seek them in migrant traps like Forest Park and Tower Grove Park. Some of the local nesters, however, are more easily found on their breeding grounds and are almost always located first by song. The first full week in May is usually the best time to find large numbers of warblers (and other migrant songbirds), although the migration peak varies from year to year.

Blue-winged Warbler *(Vermivora pinus)*. The Blue-wing is more commonly found in nesting areas such as Busch CA than in migrant traps. It prefers edges and open areas overgrown with shrubs and small trees.

Golden-winged Warbler *(Vermivora chrysoptera)*. Its insect-like song helps locate this warbler in spring. Birds sounding like Blue-winged and Golden-winged Warblers should be identified by sight because hybrids ("Brewster's" and "Lawrence's" warblers) are possible.

Tennessee Warbler *(Vermivora peregrina)*. During the peak of spring migration the loud, staccato song of the Tennessee Warbler can be heard in nearly any residential area with large trees. A "treetop" warbler, it is usually seen well only when it comes down to find water. There are two late fall records from St. Louis, 24 November 1985 and 27 November to 4 December 1988.

Orange-crowned Warbler *(Vermivora celata)*. This unobtrusive migrant is difficult to find when sought and is usually seen when not expected. It is more common some years than others and in some years is easier to find in fall than spring.

Nashville Warbler *(Vermivora ruficapilla)*. One of the most common of the warblers that do not breed locally, the Nashville is found in a variety of habitats. It usually passes through our area with the Tennessee Warbler but is often seen foraging closer to the ground.

Northern Parula *(Parula americana)*. This nesting warbler is usually found along wooded streams and rivers. Look for it at Shaw Arboretum, Busch CA, Pere Marquette State Park, and Mark Twain NWR. In the winter of 1983-84, a male survived on peanut butter at a Belleville, Illinois feeder.

Yellow Warbler *(Dendroica petechia)*. Look for this nesting species in willows on the edges of streams and lakes, especially at Busch CA and Horseshoe Lake.

Chestnut-sided Warbler *(Dendroica pensylvanica)*. This is one of the easiest migrant warblers to find in spring, as it usually stays low in trees. In the 1800's it bred in the St. Louis area and has bred recently in parts of northern Missouri and Illinois.

Magnolia Warbler *(Dendroica magnolia)*. The Magnolia and Chestnut-sided Warblers pass through our area together in spring. Both are usually found in small trees and the lower canopy of large trees.

Cape May Warbler *(Dendroica tigrina)*. The Cape May Warbler is found high in oaks as well as low in conifers. It is seen more frequently in some years than others. The main migration route of both the Cape May and Black-throated Blue Warblers is east of St. Louis, and both species are probably more common in the eastern part of our area (e.g., Carlyle Lake) than the western part. The Cape May has been recorded four times in early winter: 1-12 December 1963 (St. Louis), 20 December 1992 (O'Fallon, Missouri), 20 November 1993 (Busch CA), and 1 January 1994 (St. Louis Co.).

Black-throated Blue Warbler *(Dendroica caerulescens)*. This is one of the few warblers that is more frequently found in fall than in spring in our area. Recently, it has been observed most often in Tower Grove Park, feeding in low branches of trees, and at Carlyle Lake.

Yellow-rumped Warbler *(Dendroica coronata)*. The most common non-breeding warbler in our area, this hardy species occurs almost anywhere with trees in early spring and fall. It is the only warbler to winter regularly in our area, where it feeds on cedar and poison ivy berries. The western form ("Audubon's Warbler") is accidental in our area.

Black-throated Green Warbler *(Dendroica virens)*. This warbler is relatively easy to find in both spring and fall. It feeds mid-height to high in both deciduous and coniferous trees.

Blackburnian Warbler *(Dendroica fusca)*. Another "treetop" warbler, the Blackburnian is probably a more common migrant than is generally thought as its high, thin song is sometimes difficult to hear.

Black-throated Green Warbler

Yellow-throated Warbler *(Dendroica dominica)*. Seldom seen in urban parks, this breeder prefers the tops of sycamores along the rivers. Look for it at Shaw Arboretum, Castlewood State Park, Busch CA, and Mark Twain NWR before the leaves completely emerge in spring.

Pine Warbler *(Dendroica pinus)*. This species breeds locally in pines at Hawn State Park. In migration it has been seen at Busch CA, Shaw Arboretum, and Forest and Tower Grove Parks.

Kirtland's Warbler *(Dendroica kirtlandii)*. This rare warbler has been recorded twice in our area, a male collected on 8 May 1885 and an individual sighted at Busch CA on 30 September 1950.

Prairie Warbler *(Dendroica discolor)*. Look and listen for nesting Prairie Warblers calling from cedar trees in fields at Shaw Arboretum and Hawn and St. Francois State Parks. It breeds only rarely in the northern part of our area and is seldom seen in migration.

Palm Warbler *(Dendroica palmarum)*. This species is easy to find in fall as well as spring. It is seen in the lower branches of trees, or elsewhere near the ground.

Bay-breasted Warbler *(Dendroica castanea)*. This large warbler feeds high in trees, where its weak song is easily missed.

Blackpoll Warbler *(Dendroica striata)*. In spring, Blackpolls are more common some years than others. They are "treetop" warblers that are more often heard than seen. They are probably more common in the eastern part of our area, such as at Carlyle Lake. In fall Blackpolls should be identified with great caution, for they are very rare and difficult to distinguish from the more common Bay-breasted Warbler.

Cerulean Warbler *(Dendroica cerulea)*. The Cerulean shares breeding habitat with the Yellow-throated Warbler and Northern Parula. During the breeding season, look for it in the tall trees of the river bottoms, such as Castlewood State Park.

Black-and-white Warbler *(Mniotilta varia)*. The Black-and-white Warbler is most often seen in migration, although it is a casual breeder in mature forests.

American Redstart *(Setophaga ruticilla)*. Redstarts breed locally in small numbers, usually in forests near water of the Mississippi and Kaskaskia River floodplains. They are easier to find as migrants, however.

Black-and-white Warbler

Prothonotary Warbler *(Protonotaria citrea)*. A local breeder that favors wet, lowland forests, this species is probably more common than generally thought, as it is seldom seen in migrant traps. Look and listen for it at Shaw Arboretum, Castlewood State Park, Mark Twain NWR, and Calhoun Point.

Worm-eating Warbler *(Helmitheros vermivorus)*. In their breeding areas Worm-eaters are found in wooded ravines and on steep hillsides. In spring, they are more commonly seen in migrant traps than many other locally breeding warblers. They nest at Shaw Arboretum, Busch CA, Weldon Spring CA, and Hawn State Park.

Swainson's Warbler *(Limnothlypis swainsonii)*. This is one of the few warblers for which the breeding range is south of St. Louis. In the summer of 1972, Swainson's Warblers apparently bred in Illinois near the mouth of the Kaskaskia River. There have been fewer than ten spring records of migrants since 1950, all between 22 April and 22 May. There is only one fall record, 16-17 September 1972 from Busch CA.

Ovenbird *(Seiurus aurocapillus)*. The Ovenbird is a widespread nesting warbler in regions of extensive upland forest, and an easy species to find in migrant traps, where it often sings.

Northern Waterthrush *(Seiurus noveboracensis)*. The Northern Waterthrush is often found in Forest and Tower Grove Parks, where it is usually seen on or near the ground. Its loud song is often heard in migration, allowing it to be easily distiguished from the next species.

Louisiana Waterthrush *(Seiurus motacilla)*. Whereas the Northern Waterthrush breeds north of St. Louis, the Louisiana is a common local breeder along wooded streams; it is only occasionally found in migrant traps in spring. Seek it at Busch CA, Weldon Spring CA, Shaw Arboretum, and creeks draining into the Mississippi River from the bluffs in Illinois.

Kentucky Warbler *(Oporornis formosus)*. Although often hard to locate, the Kentucky Warbler is a widespread breeder in the understory of mature forests, where its song is frequently heard. Look for it at Shaw Arboretum, Busch CA, Rockwoods, and wooded areas of Illinois. It also occurs regularly in migrant traps in spring.

Connecticut Warbler *(Oporornis agilis)*. This is one of the most difficult to find of the regularly occurring migrant warblers because it is rare and passes through the area in late spring when the vegetation is densest. It usually remains near the ground and is best located by its distinctive song.

Mourning Warbler *(Oporornis philadelphia)*. More common some years than others, this warbler is usually seen in the understory of migrant traps. Like the Connecticut Warbler, it has the annoying habit of singing several times, moving, and then remaining silent for a while.

[MacGillivray's Warbler *(Oporornis tolmiei)*] *Hypothetical*. There has been a single report of this species: a singing male, 21-22 May 1950 (Creve Coeur Lake).

Common Yellowthroat *(Geothlypis trichas)*. This is the most common and widespread breeding warbler in our area. It is seen in marshes, meadows, and thickets bordering water, most often below eye level. It is particularly easy to find at Marais Temps Clair.

Hooded Warbler *(Wilsonia citrina)*. This large warbler is most often encountered in migrant traps in spring, although it is also a rare breeder in our area. Its loud song reveals its presence.

Wilson's Warbler *(Wilsonia pusilla)*. Wilson's Warblers are seen regularly in spring and fall, usually in forest understory and shrubs. Unlike most warblers, it responds well to "pish-ing."

Canada Warbler *(Wilsonia canadensis)*. Like the preceding species, this warbler is most often found in the understory of the forest. It is regularly found in migrant traps and also in bottomland forests during migration.

Yellow-breasted Chat *(Icteria virens)*. The Chat is a common nesting bird that is seldom seen in migrant traps. It is found in open country with hedgerows or scattered thick cover, such as at Busch CA and Shaw Arboretum.

TANAGERS, CARDINAL, GROSBEAKS, BUNTINGS, AND DICKCISSEL

Summer Tanager *(Piranga rubra)*. Often seen in spring migration, this tanager can also be found throughout the summer and early fall in upland oak forests, edges, and glades. It is a common and characteristic bird of Missouri woodlands.

Scarlet Tanager *(Piranga olivacea)*. The Scarlet Tanager is most often seen during spring migration, but it also nests in the interior of large tracts of upland forests. Overall, it is somewhat less numerous and widespread than the Summer Tanager.

Western Tanager *(Piranga ludoviciana)*. There have been two credible reports of this western species: a female, 21 May 1966 (Shaw Arboretum) and a male, 21 August 1966 (St. Louis Co.).

Northern Cardinal *(Cardinalis cardinalis)*. The state bird of Illinois and the unofficial city bird of St. Louis, the Cardinal is one of our most common suburban and rural species.

Rose-breasted Grosbeak

Rose-breasted Grosbeak *(Pheucticus ludovicianus)*. An uncommon nesting species, mainly north of the Missouri River, this grosbeak is a common migrant in woodlands and suburbs.

Black-headed Grosbeak *(Pheucticus melanocephalus)*. Since 1970 there have been three spring records of this western species: 2 females, 20 April 1977 (Olivette); a male, 12 May 1982 (Forest Park), and a male, 21 April 1985 (University City). The five fall occurrences have been either females or immature males.

Blue Grosbeak *(Guiraca caerulea)*. Local in distribution, the Blue Grosbeak is often seen perched on utility wires in open shrubby areas with hedgerows. It has bred at Weldon Spring CA and Shaw Arboretum. There is one winter record from 4 December 1952 (St. Louis).

Lazuli Bunting *(Passerina amoena)*. Three of the records for this western species have been during spring migration, all of males: 7 May 1950 (Webster Groves), 15 May 1983 (University City), and 10 May 1984 (Forest Park). In addition, a Lazuli-Indigo hybrid occurred at Marais Temps Clair on 14 June 1980.

Indigo Bunting *(Passerina cyanea)*. This is one of our most common and widespread small birds of second-growth forests, open shrubby areas, and edges. It often perches on utility wires along roadsides, where it sings incessantly. In September and October, Indigos gather in flocks in brushy or weedy areas with sparrows.

Dickcissel *(Spiza americana)*. The Dickcissel prefers open farm country near weedy meadows and fields, where it is usually seen perched on shrubs or utility wires. It can be found at Riverlands EDA, Weldon Springs CA, and in agricultural areas of Illinois. There have been a few winter records: 23 December 1965 (Busch CA), 2 January 1983 (St. Charles Co.), and 15 March to 1 April 1986 at a feeder in St. Louis.

TOWHEES AND SPARROWS

Of the 23 species of native sparrows and towhees that have occurred in our area, only six regularly breed here. Four others bred formerly. The rest pass through our area in spring and fall, and some species winter here. October-November is the best time to see a large variety of sparrow species.

Green-tailed Towhee *(Pipilo chlorurus)*. There are two records for our area, one at Busch CA, 23 November to 26 December 1952, and another also at Busch CA, 3 February 1976, seen by a single observer.

Rufous-sided Towhee *(Pipilo erythrophthalmus)*. This common breeding bird occurs in a variety of habitats, but usually near forest edges and brushy areas. It is seen in the suburbs during migration and sometimes visits feeders in mild winters. The western form ("Spotted Towhee") has occurred in our area in winter.

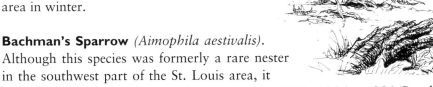

Rufous-sided Towhee

Bachman's Sparrow *(Aimophila aestivalis)*. Although this species was formerly a rare nester in the southwest part of the St. Louis area, it has only been reported on three occasions since 1950: 13 May 1956 (Busch CA), 29 April 1977 (St. Louis Co.), and 21 July 1990 (Busch CA, with no evidence of nesting).

American Tree Sparrow *(Spizella arborea)*. This cold-weather sparrow usually occurs in flocks in weedy fields. Though more common some years than others, it is normally one of the three or four most numerous winter sparrows in our area, although it is seldom seen at feeders.

Chipping Sparrow *(Spizella passerina)*. Look for nesting Chipping Sparrows in parks, cemeteries, and suburbs, particularly in conifers. It is more numerous and widespread in migration. Winter sightings should be carefully documented.

Clay-colored Sparrow *(Spizella pallida)*. One of the rarest sparrows to occur regularly in our area, the Clay-colored is sometimes found in weedy fields. Since 1988, however, it has been seen nearly every spring and fall in Tower Grove Park. Three individuals were found at Busch CA on 29 December 1963.

Field Sparrow *(Spizella pusilla)*. As its name implies, this nesting species is easy to find in overgrown weedy fields, where it perches on shrubs and small trees. In summer, Field Sparrows are easily located by their distinctive songs. St. Louis is on the northern fringe of this species' winter range, so most of our Field Sparrows depart for the winter.

Vesper Sparrow *(Pooecetes gramineus)*. This sparrow is found in short grass fields and hedgerows during migration. There are no recent breeding records, although there is one recent summer record, 7 July 1979 in St. Charles Co. The Vesper nests in northern Missouri and central Illinois.

Lark Sparrow *(Chondestes grammacus)*. Lark Sparrows nest in croplands and pastures in rural areas, but during migration they are seen in a variety of habitats. Much less common here than in western Missouri, they are most often reported from Shaw Arboretum and Busch CA.

Lark Bunting *(Calamospiza melanocorys)*. The only record of this western species is a single individual from St. Charles Co. (Mueller Road) on 5 September 1983.

Savannah Sparrow *(Passerculus sandwichensis)*. This sparrow is usually seen in migration in open grassy fields. It is likely that the subspecies seen in late April and early May, which has distinctly yellow lores, is different from the subspecies that occurs in the colder months.

[Baird's Sparrow *(Ammodramus bairdii)***]** *Hypothetical.* Although there have been several reports of this prairie species, it has not been convincingly documented because of the resemblance of the Baird's to other sparrows. Two 19th-century records reported by Widmann (1907) remain suspect.

Grasshopper Sparrow *(Ammodramus savannarum)*. This species prefers fields of dense grass or hay crops. It nests in various locations in St. Charles Co. (Riverlands EDA and Busch CA) and St. Clair Co. It is usually found by its insect-like song; watch for singing birds on grass tops or fence wires.

Henslow's Sparrow *(Ammodramus henslowii)*. This little sparrow breeds in the Experimental Prarie at Shaw Arboretum in some years, and there are some pre-1970 breeding records for St. Charles Co. It is found only rarely in migration, usually in grassy fields.

Le Conte's Sparrow *(Ammodramus leconteii)*. This migrant has been seen most often at Busch CA, but also in the dense grassy fields of Riverlands EDA, Horseshoe Lake, and Mark Twain NWR. It is more common some years than others. Because it remains well hidden in the grass, finding and observing the Le Conte's may require patient effort.

Sharp-tailed Sparrow *(Ammodramus caudacutus)*. The seldom-seen Sharp-tailed Sparrow is found most often in weeds adjacent to lakes and marshes and lakes. Look for it at Busch CA, Mark Twain NWR, and Horseshoe Lake.

Fox Sparrow *(Passerella iliaca)*. This large sparrow occurs in hedgerows and along woodland edges, usually in small numbers. It is also sometimes seen on the forest floor turning leaves like a towhee. Before leaving our area in early spring, Fox Sparrows can often be heard singing.

Song Sparrow *(Melospiza melodia)*. Nesting Song Sparrows are often found near water, but also in a wide variety of other habitats, including the suburbs. This is the most common of our native, breeding sparrows. Winter brings an influx of Song Sparrows from farther north, and they become common in weedy fields and woodland edges.

Lincoln's Sparrow *(Melospiza lincolnii)*. This secretive migrant, found in thickets and brushpiles, is often seen in Forest Park and Tower Grove Park. There are a few winter records: 18 December 1982 (Calhoun Co.), 30 January 1983 (Horseshoe Lake), and 2 January 1988 (St. Charles Co.).

Swamp Sparrow *(Melospiza georgiana)*. Swamp Sparrows are found along with Song Sparrows in wet fields and marshes, such as Marais Temps Clair and Mark Twain NWR, and in upland brushy and weedy areas. They bred in St. Charles Co. as late as 1905.

White-throated Sparrow *(Zonotrichia albicollis)*. This is one of the most commonly observed sparrows in wooded areas and at feeders in winter. It sings regularly in spring and fall.

White-crowned Sparrow *(Zonotrichia leucophrys)*. This sparrow is found in hedgerows and brushpiles and prefers more open areas than the White-throated Sparrow. It is sometimes found in migrant traps, and sings in both spring and fall.

White-throated Sparrow

Harris's Sparrow *(Zonotrichia querula)*. Of the *Zonotrichia* sparrows, this is the least common; there are seldom more than one or two reports

of this species in a year. It
has appeared in a variety
of habitats, including at feeders,
but has been seen most often at Busch
CA. It is often found in the company of
White-crowned Sparrows.

Dark-eyed Junco *(Junco hyemalis)*. This is probably our
most numerous winter-
ing sparrow. It
occurs in a
variety of habitats
throughout our area
and is a common feeder
visitor, although it usually feeds
on spilled seed *under* the feeder. The race formerly known as the "Oregon
Junco" is sometimes seen in our area.

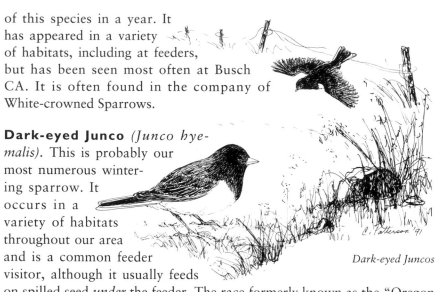

Dark-eyed Juncos

LONGSPURS AND SNOW BUNTING

McCown's Longspur *(Calcarius mccownii)*. The only record of this
species in our area was of two individuals at Busch CA, 11-16 January
1979.

Lapland Longspur *(Calcarius lapponicus)*. Although our only regular
longspur, the Lapland varies in abundance from year to year. It is easiest
to find in years of significant snow cover when it is forced to feed in gravel at the side of the road. It is usually seen in flocks, sometimes numbering
in the thousands, and often in the company of Horned Larks. Look and
listen for it at airports, in bare fields or corn stubble, or in grassy fields in
St. Charles Co., Riverlands EDA, and near Carlyle Lake.

Smith's Longspur *(Calcarius pictus)*. This transient is not seen in our
area every year. When it occurs it is usually seen in small numbers,
although flocks of up to 250 individuals have been seen in spring. Most
reports have been from short-grass areas at St. Charles Airport and St.
Charles Co. Airport. It has also been seen at Riverlands EDA, Horseshoe
Lake, and Carlyle Lake.

Chestnut-collared Longspur *(Calcarius ornatus)*. There are only three
area records for this species: 22-28 February 1957 and 14 February 1959,

both at St. Charles Airport, and 16 November 1991 in eastern St. Charles Co. Each sighting was of a single individual in company of Lapland Longspurs.

Snow Bunting *(Plectrophenax nivalis)*. Most sightings of this open field bird have occurred when there was heavy snow cover, often in company of Lapland Longspurs or Horned Larks. Usually fewer than five individuals are seen at a time, but flocks of up to 70 have occurred. Look for it in the flat agricultural areas of eastern St. Charles Co. and Illinois.

BOBOLINK, BLACKBIRDS, MEADOWLARKS, AND ORIOLES

Bobolink *(Dolichonyx oryzivorus)*. This transient passes through our area quickly in spring, when it is usually found in alfalfa and clover fields; males usually precede females. Listen for its distinctive song. In fall, flocks are easily overlooked because of the dramatic change in plumage.

Red-winged Blackbird *(Agelaius phoeniceus)*. The Red-wing breeds almost anywhere near water. In winter it has been found in flocks numbering hundreds of thousands at and around Marais Temps Clair, Mark Twain NWR, the Mississippi River floodplain east of St. Louis, and Carlyle Lake.

Eastern Meadowlark *(Sturnella magna)*. This is the common meadowlark of agricultural fields, pastures, and grasslands. It is easy to find at Riverlands EDA, Busch CA, and agricultural areas of Illinois.

Western Meadowlark *(Sturnella neglecta)*. Western and Eastern Meadowlarks are difficult to distinguish from each other by plumage and share the same habitat. Western Meadowlarks do not breed in the area and are most easy to find in March, when they sing in migration. In winter, they may be more common than generally thought; listen for call notes as well as song.

Yellow-headed Blackbird *(Xanthocephalus xanthocephalus)*. Most reports are of one or two individuals from marshy habitat at Marais Temps Clair, Busch CA, Horseshoe Lake, and Riverlands EDA. There are a few confirmed nesting records for this species in our area.

Rusty Blackbird *(Euphagus carolinus)*. This blackbird favors moist lowland woods and fields and is sometimes seen in small numbers in mixed flocks of other blackbirds in winter. Although most often encountered in rural areas, flocks are sometimes found in suburbs and parks.

Brewer's Blackbird *(Euphagus cyanocephalus)*. Small flocks of this open-country blackbird are sometimes found on mudflats, fields, and roadsides, alone or with other blackbirds. It must be distinguished with care from both the Rusty Blackbird and the Common Grackle.

Great-tailed Grackle *(Quiscalus mexicanus)*. Two recent sightings of this species may signify the beginning of a range expansion into our area. Both were from agricultural regions of St. Charles Co.: a female, 10 December 1989 (single observer); and two males, 15 November 1991. The only previous record is from 4 January 1958, also in St. Charles Co. (originally reported as a Boat-tailed Grackle, but this was before the taxonomic split of the two large grackles).

Common Grackle *(Quiscalus quiscula)*. This is the common, widespread grackle of our area. In winter, Grackles often congregate in large flocks; they may be absent from one area and abundant in another.

Brown-headed Cowbird *(Molothrus ater)*. Cowbirds are common in most habitats except areas of extensive undisturbed forest. They become more local in winter, joining other blackbirds in flocks in open country. Cowbirds lay their eggs in the nests of other songbirds and are one cause of the decrease in numbers of some of our locally breeding warblers.

Orchard Oriole *(Icterus spurius)*. Orchard Orioles are found along fencerows, in overgrown shrubby areas, in open country with scattered large trees, and around rural residences. There is one winter record, a male at Carlyle Lake on 15 December 1982.

Northern Oriole *(Icterus galbula)*. This oriole is found in open woodlands, parks, and sometimes residential areas. There are a few records of late stragglers into early winter. A female of the western form ("Bullock's" Oriole) was reported by a single observer from Fort Kaskaskia on 3 May 1986.

FINCHES

Most of the species listed below are "winter finches" in that they are only seen in the area in winter. Only the American Goldfinch and House Finch are year-round residents.

[Pine Grosbeak *(Pinicola enucleator)*] *Hypothetical*. There have been two reports of this species, both by single observers: 18 January 1964 and 11 March 1982.

Purple Finch *(Carpodacus purpureus).* This inconspicuous and quiet winter finch is variable in abundance from year to year. It is frequently seen at feeders, and also in wooded areas, often at the tops of food-source trees like sweetgum and sycamore. During spring migration, males sing vigorously.

House Finch *(Carpodacus mexicanus).* The first area House Finch occurred at a feeder on 23 November 1974 in Webster Groves. This was followed by sightings of individual birds on 1 December 1977 in Glendale and 16 January 1983 in University City, both at feeders. The first nesting was recorded in Jennings in the summer of 1983. During the next five years the species became established throughout St. Louis, its suburbs, and small towns in rural areas. It now breeds in parks and many suburban and urban neighborhoods, where it has become one of the most common visitors at feeders, sometimes in groups exceeding 20 birds. It is often mistaken for the Purple Finch by people with older identification guides.

Red Crossbill *(Loxia curvirostra).* Both crossbills are irregular winter visitors. Most years they are not observed at all, but some years there are several reports, usually of flocks numbering less than ten. The Red Crossbill is one of the most erratic and unpredictable in distribution of North American birds. It favors pines, spruces, and hemlocks; thus, most reports are from places with ornamental conifers. Many winter sightings have been from Shaw Arboretum, and in 1972, birds were seen throughout the summer at this location.

White-winged Crossbill *(Loxia leucoptera).* See previous species. The White-winged Crossbill favors spruces and hemlocks, so it is most likely to occur in older, well-planted residential neighborhoods and cemeteries. Like the Red Crossbill, it sometimes visits feeders.

Common Redpoll *(Carduelis flammea).* Redpolls occurs rarely and erratically. Most years there are no reports, but some years bring small flocks to the area. Watch for it at feeders, along gravel roadsides, in fields and brushy habitat in open country, and any place with flocks of Goldfinches and Siskins.

Pine Siskin *(Carduelis pinus).* This is another erratic northern finch; some years only one or two birds are seen, other years Siskins may be fairly common. More than 2000 were seen in Bellefontaine Cemetery in December, 1965. Look for it in conifers, sweetgum trees, weedy fields, and thistle feeders, where it is often found with Goldfinches. Listen for its distinctive voice.

American Goldfinch *(Carduelis tristis)*. The Goldfinch is a widespread resident that occurs in thistle fields, woodland edges, parks, and suburbs. It is a common feeder visitor year round.

Evening Grosbeak *(Coccothraustes vespertinus)*. This large grosbeak is an erratic visitor from the north. Some winters none are seen, other years a few individuals are reported, but in irruption years they can be quite numerous. Flocks numbering 30-60 were seen in 1934 and 1962. Although they are sometimes seen in sweetgum, ash, and box elder trees, eating seeds and buds, they are most commonly discovered at feeders.

American Goldfinch

WEAVERS

House Sparrow
(Passer domesticus)
Introduced. The House Sparrow was first observed in St. Louis in 1870 after having been introduced into the United States in 1850. It is now found nearly anywhere inhabited by humans.

Eurasian Tree Sparrow *(Passer montanus) Introduced.* Taxonomically last but certainly not least, the "ETS" has been a special resident of the St. Louis area since 1870 (see **INTRODUCTION**). Some specific locations to seek the species are given below.

Within the city of St. Louis, the most consistent area for finding the ETS has been southwest of Forest Park, an area bordered roughly by Wise Avenue on the north, Bellevue Avenue on the west, a few blocks south of Dale Avenue on the south, and a few blocks east of McCausland Avenue on the east (check any visible feeders in this residential neighborhood). They are also seen along the Mississippi River, such as at North Riverfront Park and East Grand Boulevard (near grain elevators and the sewage treatment plant). Curiously, they are seldom encountered in Forest and Tower Grove Parks.

In St. Louis Co., a productive area is along Missouri Bottom Road and Aubuchon Road, in the Missouri River floodplain, northwest of the metropolitan area. This area is easily accessible from Lambert Airport. Take I-70 west, exit at the Earth City Expressway just before the Missouri River, and head north. After crossing MO-370, check any farmyards and fencerows. Further east along the Missouri River, Sioux Passage County Park offers an additional opportunity.

The ETS is also found routinely in the floodplain of eastern St. Charles Co. Some consistent areas include trees near parking areas at Marais Temps Clair, along Weber Lake, Dwiggins, and Saale Roads, along the Mississippi River at the end of Grafton Ferry Road, and at Riverlands EDA.

In Illinois, the ETS can be found around Horseshoe Lake, especially along Layton Road and on Walker's Island. In Calhoun County, just after disembarking from the Brussels Ferry, check the riverfront road west of the ferry landing.

Golden-crowned Kinglet

GLOSSARY OF NAMED PLACES, LOCAL JARGON, AND ABBREVIATIONS

Named Place or Abbreviation	Location or Definition
Alta Villa	access to Mississippi R., off MO-94, north of West Alton, MO
Alton	city in Madison Co., IL, north of St. Louis
Alton dam	prior to 1990, Dam No. 26, Mississippi R. at Alton; now replaced by the Melvin Price Dam, No. 26R, 2 miles downstream (east) of the former location
Alton Lake, Alton Pool	Mississippi R. upstream (west) of dam to Grafton
Alton power plant	on IL-143, northeast of Melvin Price Dam
A. O. U.	American Ornithologists Union, organization of professional ornithologists
"arch"	Gateway Arch, Jefferson National Expansion Memorial, downtown St. Louis, MO
archery (range)	at Busch Conservation Area
Baldwin Lake	part of Kaskaskia River State Fish and Wildlife Area, St. Clair Co. and Randolph Co., IDC, IL; cooling pond for power plant
Bellefontaine Cemetery	northern St. Louis city; final resting place of Capt. William Clark (of Clark's Grebe and Clark's Nutcracker)
Bend Road, Big Bend Road	access to Horseshoe Lk., off IL hwy. 203 on west side of lake; not to be confused with St. Louis Co.'s Big Bend Blvd./Rd.
Bim's Place	access to Swan Lake in Mark Twain NWR, Calhoun Co., IL
birder	a person who enjoys observing birds
birding	what nonbirders often call "bird-watching"

Named Place or Abbreviation	Location or Definition
Blanchette Memorial Bridge	I-70 crossing of Missouri R. at St. Charles
"the brushpile"	formerly, a brushpile in the northwest corner of Tower Grove Park; now, the location of the Robert and Martha Gaddy Wild Bird Garden
Brussels Ferry	Illinois R., between Jersey and Calhoun Cos., just west of Grafton
"burnt-out house"	an access to Horseshoe Lake off IL-111 near the intersection of Sand Prairie Rd.
Busch (Conservation Area) CA	August A. Busch Memorial Conservation Area, MDC, state hwy. 94 and Co. hwy. D, St. Charles Co., MO
CA	Conservation Area (MDC, formerly Wildlife Area); not California
Calhoun Co.	IL, between Mississippi and Illinois Rivers
Calhoun Point	confluence of Illinois and Mississippi Rivers, Calhoun Co., IL
Carlyle Lake	primarily in Clinton Co., IL, 50 miles east of St. Louis
Castlewood State Park	west St. Louis Co., on Meramec River
Chain of Rocks	Dam No. 27 on Mississippi River south of I-270 bridge; most birding records refer to sandbars on IL side
CBC	Christmas Bird Count
Clarence Cannon NWR	Pike Co., MO. The refuge is part of the Annada Division of the Mark Twain NWR
Clark Bridge	US-67 crossing of Mississippi R. at Alton
Co., Cos.	county, counties
Comfort Woods	James E. Comfort Forest at Busch CA
Creve Coeur Lake	oxbow lake of Missouri R., west St. Louis Co., bordered by Creve Coeur County Park

Named Place or Abbreviation	Location or Definition
cypress tree circle	in east-central Tower Grove Park
Daniel Boone Bridge	I-64 crossing of the Missouri R. at Chesterfield
"the dredge"	a barge and dredging operation in Horseshoe Lake at the end of Layton Rd.
Eagle Park marsh	unofficial name of the marsh west of IL hwy. 203 on Eagle Park Rd.
equipment shed	refers either to shed at Marais Temps Clair CA or Mark Twain NWR at Swan Lake
ETS	local nickname for the Eurasian Tree Sparrow
Forest Park	in St. Louis city, north of I-64/US-40
Fort Kaskaskia (State Historic Site)	Randolph Co., IL
Franklin Co.	MO, west of St. Louis Co. along I-44
Gilbert Lake	oxbow lake along Illinois R. in Jersey Co.; part of Mark Twain NWR
Golden Eagle Ferry	Mississippi R., between Calhoun Co., IL, and St. Charles Co., MO
Great River Road	IL-100, west of Alton; scenic drive along the Mississippi R. and Illinois R. bluffs; also IL-143 and IL-3 east and south of Alton
Harbor Point (Yacht Club)	access to Mississippi R., off MO hwy. 94, north of West Alton, MO
Hawn State Park	MO, Ste. Genevieve Co.
Hawthorne St.	access to Mississippi R. off IL hwy. 3 near Wood River
Hayford Rd	off Hwy. B, St. Charles Co., MO
Hazlet State Park	Eldon Hazlet State Park, on Carlyle Lk., Clinton Co., IL
Hickory Hollow	picnic area and access to Carlyle Lake

Named Place or Abbreviation	Location or Definition
Holten State Park	Frank Holten State Park, St. Clair Co., IL
Horseshoe Lake	Madison Co., IL; includes Horseshoe Lake, Horseshoe Lake State Park, and private lands on west side of the lake
hotline	an informal but organized system among birders to inform each other by telephone of any rare birds that have been spotted in the area
hwy.	highway
I-44, I-55 I-255, I-64, I-70, I-270	U. S. interstate highways
IDC	Illinois Department of Conservation
IL	Illinois
IL-3, IL-111, IL-124, IL-203, etc.	Illinois state highways
Jefferson Barracks	St. Louis Co. Park and National Cemetery, south St. Louis Co., along Mississippi R. north of I-255 bridge
Jefferson Co.	MO, south of St. Louis
Jersey Co.	IL, north of Mississippi River
(John F.) Kennedy Forest	southwest corner of Forest Park, city of St. Louis
Lk.	Lake
Lambert Field	Lambert St. Louis International Airport, along I-70, St. Louis Co.
Layton Road	access to Horseshoe Lk., off (Big) Bend Rd.; ends at Horseshoe Lake State Park
levees, levee region	leveed Mississippi R. floodplain in Monroe Co., IL, south of I-255 (Jefferson Barracks) bridge to just south of Fults
Little Creve Coeur Lake	seasonally wet lowlands west of Creve Coeur Lk. and Creve Coeur Mill Rd.; now largely developed

Named Place or Abbreviation	Location or Definition
Macoupin Co.	IL, northeast of St. Louis
Madison Co.	IL, east of St. Louis
Marais Temps Clair ("MTC")	oxbow lake; presently an MDC CA, prior to the mid 1980's a private duck hunting club; St. Charles Co., MO
Mark Twain NWR	Calhoun and Jersey Cos., IL, along Illinois R.
MDC	Missouri Department of Conservation
Melvin Price Dam	Dam No. 26R, Mississippi R.; see Alton dam and Riverlands EDA
Missouri Botanical Garden	city of St. Louis; ("Shaw's Garden")
MO	Missouri
MO-79, MO-94, MO-141, etc.	Missouri state highways
Monroe Co.	IL, east and south of St. Louis
Moredock Lake	Monroe Co., IL
Mueller Rd. (lagoon)	north of St. Charles, between Airport Rd. and Boschertown Rd., off Co. hwy. B; usually refers to sewage lagoon or adjacent ballfields; St. Charles Co., MO
Nature Line	a recorded telephone message announcing recent interesting bird sightings; sponsored by WGNSS
Nature Notes	journal of the WGNSS
NWR	National Wildlife Refuge
O'Fallon, IL	on I-64, not to be confused with O'Fallon, MO
O'Fallon, MO	on I-70, not to be confused with O'Fallon, IL
Orchard Farm	town in eastern St. Charles Co., MO; center of a CBC
Ozarks	forested hill region south and west of St. Louis

Named Place or Abbreviation	Location or Definition
passerines	birds of the order Passeriformes, which includes "songbirds" (thrushes, warblers, finches), as well as jays, crows, flycatchers, sparrows, and others
Pere Marquette (State Park)	Pere Marquette State Park, Jersey Co., IL, west of Alton; center of a CBC
"pishing"	a "pish" noise birders make to attract birds
Poplar St. Bridge	I-55/64/70 crossing of Mississippi R. in downtown St. Louis
Portage Des Sioux	town in eastern St. Charles Co., MO, on Mississippi R.
pump station	access to Swan Lake in Mark Twain NWR, Calhoun Co., IL
R.	River
Randolph Co.	IL, south of St. Louis
Riverlands EDA (Environmental Demonstration Area) ...	U. S. Army Corps of Engineers; area mostly upriver (west) of Melvin Price Dam to US-67, on MO side of Mississippi R.
Rockwoods (Reservation)	MDC, west St. Louis Co.
St. Charles Co.	MO, west and north of St. Louis, between Mississippi and Missouri rivers
St. Charles Airport	on Co. hwy. B, St. Charles Co.
St. Charles Co. Airport	formerly Smartt Field, north of Marais Temps Clair
St. Clair Co.	IL, southeast of St. Louis
St. Francois State Park	MO, St. Francois Co.
St. Louis Co.	MO, excludes St. Louis city
Scott Air Force Base	St. Clair Co., IL
Shanks (Ted) CA	MDC, Pike Co., MO

Named Place or Abbreviation	Location or Definition
Shaw Arboretum	Missouri Botanical Garden Arboretum, Gray Summit, Franklin Co., MO; west on I-44 from St. Louis
"Shaw's Garden"	Missouri Botanical Garden
"Shop Lake"	Hampton Memorial Lake at Busch CA
spillway	usually refers to dam at Carlyle Lake
Stump Lake	oxbow lake along Illinois R. in Jersey Co., IL, opposite entrance to Pere Marquette State Park
Swan Lake	oxbow lake along Illinois R. in Calhoun Co., IL; part of Mark Twain NWR
Teal Pond	Riverlands EDA; the first pond on the right (south) past entrance
"the (St. Louis) area"	the region within 50 miles of the St. Louis city limits
Tower Grove Park	in St. Louis city; usually refers to northwest corner of park
Tyson Research Center	I-44 at Antire Rd, west St. Louis Co.; private (Washington University)
US-40, US-50, etc.	U. S. (federal) highways
Valley Sailing Association	access to Mississippi R., along MO-94 in St. Charles Co.
the "volcano"	access to Swan Lake in Mark Twain NWR, Calhoun Co., IL
Walker's Island	island in Horseshoe Lk.
Weldon Spring	town in St. Charles Co., MO; site of MDC CA, state hwy. 94 and Co. hwy. D; center of a CBC
Webster Groves	city in St. Louis Co.
Winfield dam	Dam No. 25 on Mississippi R. at Winfield, MO
WGNSS	Webster Groves Nature Study Society (pronounced "wigness")

Field Sparrow atop purple coneflower

he following pages contain bar graphs depicting the seasonal occurrence and relative abundance of 343 species of birds that have been seen in the St. Louis area from 1940 through December 1993. Twenty-seven additional species are discussed in the **SPECIES ACCOUNTS** but not included in the bar graphs because they are *extinct* (2: Carolina Parakeet, Passenger Pigeon), *extirpated* (7: Trumpeter Swan, Swallow-tailed Kite, Greater Prairie-Chicken, Whooping Crane, Eskimo Curlew, Long-billed Curlew, Ivory-billed Woodpecker), *accidental* before 1940 (4: Fulvous Whistling-Duck, King Eider, Harlequin Duck, Brown-headed Nuthatch), *hypothetical* (12: Black-bellied Whistling-Duck, Reddish Egret, Roseate Spoonbill, Barnacle Goose, Tufted Duck, Ferruginous Hawk, Purple Sandpiper, Black-billed Magpie, Northern Shrike, MacGillivray's Warbler, Baird's Sparrow, Pine Grosbeak), or *introduced* but not established (2: Ringed Turtle-Dove, Monk Parakeet).

Relative Abundance. Relative abundance is described by six terms: *Common* or *abundant, Fairly common, Uncommon, Rare, Casual,* and *Accidental.* These terms are used here in a manner generally consistent with usage in checklists and other books of this type for other parts of the country. However, because birders' usage of terms like *Uncommon* and *Casual* is somewhat different from the meanings of these terms in other contexts, the terms are defined below. The important point about these terms is that they refer to the probability of a single party of one or more birders observing the species in its *preferred habitat* at a certain time of year; they do not refer to the total number of individuals of the species that occur in the St. Louis area at a given time. Some numerical probabilities are given below, but these are only approximations. Although we have made a sincere attempt to apply the various terms consistently, it is difficult to uniformly apply terms such as *Fairly common* to hawks, rails, and flycatchers alike.

Common or abundant. This category makes no distinction between species that occur in large numbers (e.g., House Sparrows) and species that occur in smaller numbers but are simply easy to find (e.g., Great Blue Herons). Swainson's Thrushes are *Common or abundant* in early May because if you spend several hours seeking a Swainson's Thrush in its preferred habitat on May 10 your chance of seeing one is greater than 90%.

Fairly common. A species that is *Fairly common* is sometimes difficult to find and can be missed entirely when you most want to find it (e.g., Eurasian Tree Sparrow). Semipalmated Sandpipers are *Fairly common* in early September, which means that during this time a thorough search of mudflats containing shorebirds will yield a Semipalmated Sandpiper more than 50% of the time.

Uncommon. Wild Turkeys are *Uncommon* throughout the year because if you spend several hours seeking a turkey in its preferred habitat your chance of seeing or hearing one is less than about one in four (25%). They're there, but most of the time you won't encounter them.

Rare. A species that is never more common than *Rare* during the course of a year is seen on one or a few occasions most years by someone (e.g., Clay-colored Sparrow). Brown Thrashers are *Rare* in winter because if you participate in the same Christmas Bird Count every year you will probably see only about one in ten years (10%).

Casual. Species that are *Casual* are only occasional visitors to the St. Louis area and most years are not seen at all by anyone. Snowy Owls are *Casual* in winter (and have never been observed other times of the year).

Accidental. If during a particular season of the year there have been less than five records or occurrences of the species since 1940, it is *Accidental* for that season. The Rock Wren is *Accidental* because it has only been seen twice. The occurrence of a group of individuals of a species at the same place at the same time is regarded as a single occurrence. On the bar graphs, each *Accidental* record is indicated by a dot if the bird(s) remained for less than a week. When birds lingered for longer than a week, two dots indicating the first and last date observed are indicated with a line connecting them. All accidental records are discussed in the SPECIES ACCOUNTS.

Dashed lines. Some species are not consistent in their occurrence from year to year. Pine Siskins are a good example because they may be at nearly every feeder in some years but are hardly seen at all in other years. Snow Buntings are usually seen only in years when snow cover forces them this far south. In the bar graphs, a dashed line indicates that the probability of seeing the species in some years is higher than indicated. See **SPECIES ACCOUNTS** for further discussion.

Preferred habitat. The term "preferred habitat" used above is not a well-defined term and cannot be applied consistently from species to species. Operationally, preferred habitat means the places a species is usually seen by birders who want to see it. Thus, rather specific locales may be the preferred habitat. For the Swainson's Thrush, places like Tower Grove Park and Forest Park are preferred habitat in spring whereas Riverlands EDA is not because most of this area is not favorable habitat for thrushes any time of year. A mudflat full of shorebirds is preferred habitat for Semipalmated Sandpipers. For hawks, a fence post may be a preferred habitat, whereas a feeder with sunflower seeds is the preferred habitat for Evening Grosbeaks. In dry years there may be very little preferred habitat anywhere in the area for shorebirds and rails.

American Kestrel and its preferred habitat

Resident and breeding species. Certain resident species (e.g., Wild Turkey) are often easier to find at some times of the year than others because of seasonal changes in behavior (breeding, flocking, or communal roosting). Similarly, many breeding passerines (e.g., Yellow-throated Warbler) are difficult to see or hear after they begin breeding because they do not sing as frequently and they spend their time in areas not easily accessible to birders. In general, the bar graphs do not reflect these particular variations in probability of being observed. Also, the bar graphs do not reflect that some species are often seen in flocks of several to many individuals (Canvasback, Cedar Waxwing), whereas other species are almost always seen individually or in pairs (Belted Kingfisher, Solitary Vireo). These characteristics are discussed in the **SPECIES ACCOUNTS**.

If a species has been known to breed in the St. Louis area since 1940, an asterisk (*) appears on the right edge of the bar graphs. If it bred prior to 1940, or if its present breeding status is unknown, a question mark (?) appears.

A Final Caution. The information provided by these bar graphs is not perfectly accurate. The St. Louis area is large and the distribution of species and weather is not uniform over the area. Some species are more common in the Illinois portion of the area than in Missouri, and vice versa. Migrating birds may take a week or more to pass through the area, so the distribution in the northern part of the area may be quite different on a given day than in the south. Because the birders are concentrated toward the center of the area, there is a central bias, and some regions of the area have not been well birded. The seasonal distribution of some species is not well known. This problem is probably worst for the uncommon and fairly common passerines in fall, and some question marks occur in the body of the bar graphs to indicate this uncertainty. Finally, there are undoubtedly some unintended errors and inconsistencies. The authors appreciate and solicit comments from readers regarding any misrepresentations and errors for future editions of this book. The authors also encourage observers to document sightings of any species indicated here as *Casual* or *Accidental*, or for which there are no previous records for a particular season, in order to keep these classifications current. Information on rare bird documentation can be obtained from:

Mr. Dick Anderson
1147 Grenshaw Drive
St. Louis, MO 63137

Mr. Randy Korotev
800 Oakbrook Lane
St. Louis, MO 63132

Brown Thrasher: Common in summer, rare in winter

KEY TO SEASONAL OCCURRENCE BAR GRAPHS

In its preferred habitat, the species is

Common or abundant

Fairly common

Uncommon; easily missed

Rare; sparingly recorded

Casual; occasional visitor; few records

Accidental (<5 records for a season since 1940)
An individual or group of birds occurred on one to a few days
between 1940 and 1970   O
since 1970   ●
An individual or group of birds remained for more than one week ●———●

Indicates that in some years the species is more common than indicated   - - - - - - - -

Status not well known   ?

Far right column
Has bred in area since 1970   ✳

Formerly bred in area (1940-1970) or may breed presently
(breeding suspected, but not confirmed)   ?

RED-THROATED LOON TO WHITE-FACED IBIS

	Jan	Feb	Mar	Apr	May	Jun	Jul	Aug	Sep	Oct	Nov	Dec
Red-throated Loon												
Pacific Loon												
Common Loon												
Pied-billed Grebe												*
Horned Grebe												
Red-necked Grebe												o
Eared Grebe												
Western Grebe												
Clark's Grebe												
Band-rumped Storm-Petrel												
American White Pelican												
Double-crested Cormorant												*
Neotropic Cormorant												
Anhinga												
American Bittern												*
Least Bittern												*
Great Blue Heron												*
Great Egret												*
Snowy Egret												*
Little Blue Heron												*
Tricolored Heron												
Cattle Egret												*
Green Heron												*
Black-crowned Night-Heron												*
Yellow-crowned Night-Heron												*
White Ibis												
Glossy Ibis												
White-faced Ibis	*plegadis* sp?											

Notes: _____

_____

_____

_____

_____

WOOD STORK TO WHITE-WINGED SCOTER

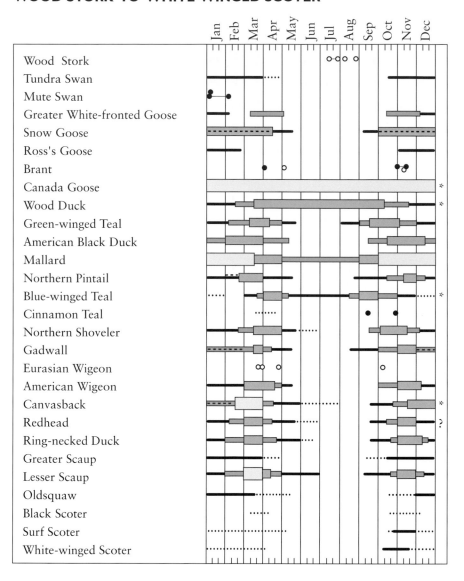

	Jan	Feb	Mar	Apr	May	Jun	Jul	Aug	Sep	Oct	Nov	Dec
Wood Stork												
Tundra Swan												
Mute Swan												
Greater White-fronted Goose												
Snow Goose												
Ross's Goose												
Brant												
Canada Goose												
Wood Duck												
Green-winged Teal												
American Black Duck												
Mallard												
Northern Pintail												
Blue-winged Teal												
Cinnamon Teal												
Northern Shoveler												
Gadwall												
Eurasian Wigeon												
American Wigeon												
Canvasback												
Redhead												
Ring-necked Duck												
Greater Scaup												
Lesser Scaup												
Oldsquaw												
Black Scoter												
Surf Scoter												
White-winged Scoter												

ABBREVIATED KEY

In its preferred habitat, the species is

Common or abundant	▨	Rare; sparingly recorded	▬
Fairly common	▨	Casual; occasional visitor; few records	··········
Uncommon; easily missed	▤	Accidental	● ○

COMMON GOLDENEYE TO PRAIRIE FALCON

Jan
Feb
Mar
Apr
May
Jun
Jul
Aug
Sep
Oct
Nov
Dec
Common Goldeneye
Barrow's Goldeneye
Bufflehead
Hooded Merganser *
Common Merganser
Red-breasted Merganser
Ruddy Duck *
Black Vulture
Turkey Vulture *
Osprey
Mississippi Kite *
Bald Eagle *
Northern Harrier ?
Sharp-shinned Hawk
Cooper's Hawk *
Northern Goshawk
Red-shouldered Hawk *
Broad-winged Hawk *
Swainson's Hawk
Red-tailed Hawk *
Rough-legged Hawk
Golden Eagle
American Kestrel *
Merlin
Peregrine Falcon *
Prairie Falcon

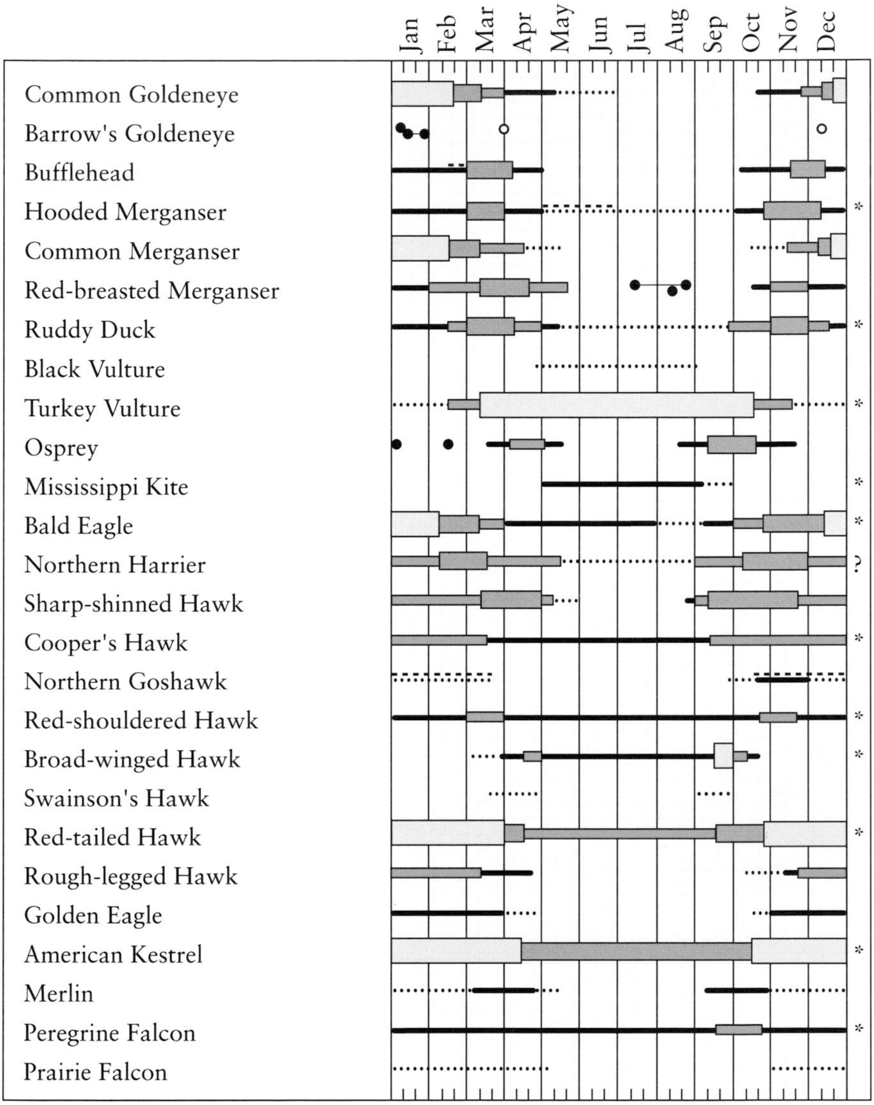

Notes

RING-NECKED PHEASANT TO SPOTTED SANDPIPER

	Jan	Feb	Mar	Apr	May	Jun	Jul	Aug	Sep	Oct	Nov	Dec
Ring-necked Pheasant												*
Ruffed Grouse												?
Wild Turkey												*
Northern Bobwhite												*
Yellow Rail												
Black Rail								o				
King Rail												*
Virginia Rail					?							*
Sora												
Purple Gallinule									o			
Common Moorhen												*
American Coot												*
Sandhill Crane												
Black-bellied Plover												
American Golden-Plover												
Semipalmated Plover												
Piping Plover												
Killdeer												*
Black-necked Stilt												?
American Avocet												
Greater Yellowlegs												
Lesser Yellowlegs												
Solitary Sandpiper												
Willet												
Spotted Sandpiper												*

ABBREVIATED KEY

In its preferred habitat, the species is

Common or abundant		Rare; sparingly recorded	━━━
Fairly common		Casual; occasional visitor; few records	········
Uncommon; easily missed		Accidental	● o

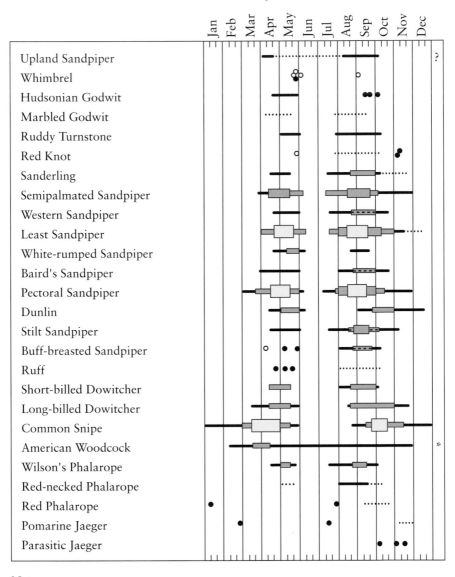

	Jan	Feb	Mar	Apr	May	Jun	Jul	Aug	Sep	Oct	Nov	Dec
Upland Sandpiper												
Whimbrel												
Hudsonian Godwit												
Marbled Godwit												
Ruddy Turnstone												
Red Knot												
Sanderling												
Semipalmated Sandpiper												
Western Sandpiper												
Least Sandpiper												
White-rumped Sandpiper												
Baird's Sandpiper												
Pectoral Sandpiper												
Dunlin												
Stilt Sandpiper												
Buff-breasted Sandpiper												
Ruff												
Short-billed Dowitcher												
Long-billed Dowitcher												
Common Snipe												
American Woodcock												
Wilson's Phalarope												
Red-necked Phalarope												
Red Phalarope												
Pomarine Jaeger												
Parasitic Jaeger												

Notes _____

_____

_____

_____

_____

Months: Jan Feb Mar Apr May Jun Jul Aug Sep Oct Nov Dec

- Laughing Gull
- Franklin's Gull
- Little Gull
- Common Black-headed Gull
- Bonaparte's Gull
- Mew Gull
- Ring-billed Gull
- California Gull
- Herring Gull
- Thayer's Gull
- Iceland Gull
- Lesser Black-backed Gull
- Slaty-backed Gull
- Glaucous Gull
- Great Black-backed Gull
- Black-legged Kittiwake
- Ross's Gull
- Sabine's Gull
- Caspian Tern
- Common Tern
- Forster's Tern
- Least Tern
- Black Tern
- Rock Dove
- Mourning Dove
- Black-billed Cuckoo
- Yellow-billed Cuckoo

ABBREVIATED KEY

In its preferred habitat, the species is

Common or abundant	
Fairly common	
Uncommon; easily missed	

Rare; sparingly recorded	
Casual; occasional visitor; few records	
Accidental	• ○

BARN OWL TO LEAST FLYCATCHER

Species	Jan	Feb	Mar	Apr	May	Jun	Jul	Aug	Sep	Oct	Nov	Dec	
Barn Owl													?
Eastern Screech-Owl													*
Great Horned Owl													*
Snowy Owl													
Barred Owl													*
Long-eared Owl													*
Short-eared Owl													
Northern Saw-whet Owl													?
Common Nighthawk													*
Chuck-will's-widow													*
Whip-poor-will													*
Chimney Swift													*
Ruby-throated Hummingbird													*
Belted Kingfisher													*
Red-headed Woodpecker													*
Red-bellied Woodpecker													*
Yellow-bellied Sapsucker													
Downy Woodpecker													*
Hairy Woodpecker													*
Northern Flicker													*
Pileated Woodpecker													*
Olive-sided Flycatcher													
Eastern Wood-Pewee													*
Yellow-bellied Flycatcher													
Acadian Flycatcher													*
Alder Flycatcher											?			
Willow Flycatcher													*
Least Flycatcher													

Notes _____

_____

_____

_____

_____

EASTERN PHOEBE TO BROWN CREEPER

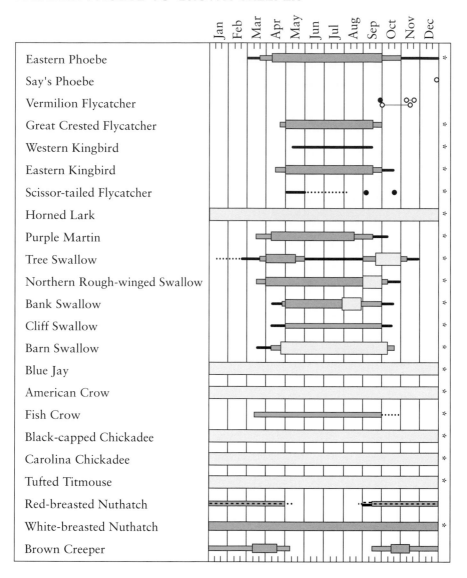

ABBREVIATED KEY

In its preferred habitat, the species is

Common or abundant		Rare; sparingly recorded		▬▬▬
Fairly common		Casual; occasional visitor; few records		··········
Uncommon; easily missed		Accidental		● ○

ROCK WREN TO EUROPEAN STARLING

	Jan	Feb	Mar	Apr	May	Jun	Jul	Aug	Sep	Oct	Nov	Dec
Rock Wren										●	●	
Carolina Wren												*
Bewick's Wren												*
House Wren												*
Winter Wren												
Sedge Wren											♂	*
Marsh Wren											?	
Golden-crowned Kinglet												
Ruby-crowned Kinglet												
Blue-gray Gnatcatcher												*
Eastern Bluebird												
Veery												
Gray-cheeked Thrush												
Swainson's Thrush												
Hermit Thrush												
Wood Thrush												*
American Robin												*
Varied Thrush										●		
Gray Catbird												*
Northern Mockingbird												*
Brown Thrasher												*
American Pipit												
Sprague's Pipit									●			
Bohemian Waxwing												
Cedar Waxwing												*
Loggerhead Shrike												*
European Starling												*

Notes _____

_____

_____

_____

_____

WHITE EYED VIREO TO BLACKPOLL WARBLER

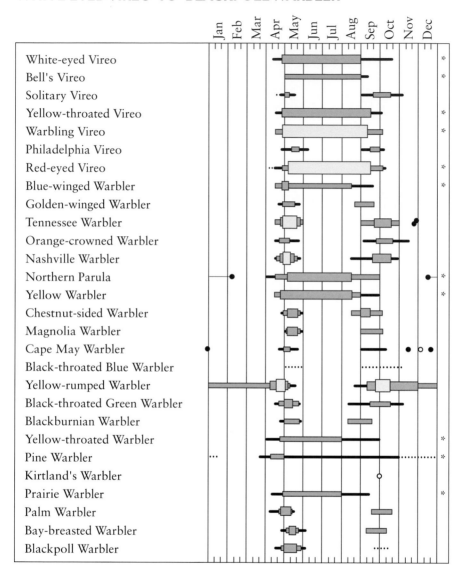

ABBREVIATED KEY

In its preferred habitat, the species is

Common or abundant	▭	Rare; sparingly recorded	▬
Fairly common	▬	Casual; occasional visitor; few records	·········
Uncommon; easily missed	▭	Accidental	● ○

CERULEAN WARBLER TO INDIGO BUNTING

	Jan	Feb	Mar	Apr	May	Jun	Jul	Aug	Sep	Oct	Nov	Dec	
Cerulean Warbler													*
Black-and-white Warbler													*
American Redstart													*
Prothonotary Warbler													*
Worm-eating Warbler													*
Swainson's Warbler													?
Ovenbird													*
Northern Waterthrush													
Louisiana Waterthrush													*
Kentucky Warbler													*
Connecticut Warbler													
Mourning Warbler													
Common Yellowthroat													*
Hooded Warbler													*
Wilson's Warbler													
Canada Warbler													
Yellow-breasted Chat													*
Summer Tanager													*
Scarlet Tanager													*
Western Tanager													
Northern Cardinal													*
Rose-breasted Grosbeak													*
Black-headed Grosbeak													
Blue Grosbeak													*
Lazuli Bunting													
Indigo Bunting													*

Notes _____

_____

_____

_____

_____

DICKCISSEL TO DARK-EYED JUNCO

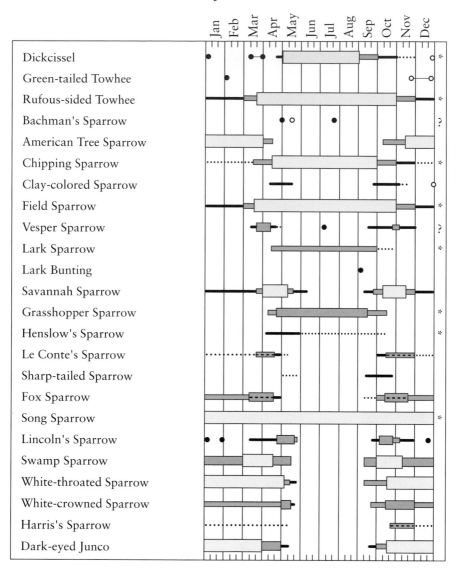

	Jan	Feb	Mar	Apr	May	Jun	Jul	Aug	Sep	Oct	Nov	Dec
Dickcissel												
Green-tailed Towhee												
Rufous-sided Towhee												
Bachman's Sparrow												
American Tree Sparrow												
Chipping Sparrow												
Clay-colored Sparrow												
Field Sparrow												
Vesper Sparrow												
Lark Sparrow												
Lark Bunting												
Savannah Sparrow												
Grasshopper Sparrow												
Henslow's Sparrow												
Le Conte's Sparrow												
Sharp-tailed Sparrow												
Fox Sparrow												
Song Sparrow												
Lincoln's Sparrow												
Swamp Sparrow												
White-throated Sparrow												
White-crowned Sparrow												
Harris's Sparrow												
Dark-eyed Junco												

ABBREVIATED KEY

In its preferred habitat, the species is

Common or abundant

Fairly common

Uncommon; easily missed

Rare; sparingly recorded

Casual; occasional visitor; few records ·········

Accidental ● ○

McCOWN'S LONGSPUR TO EURASIAN TREE SPARROW

	Jan	Feb	Mar	Apr	May	Jun	Jul	Aug	Sep	Oct	Nov	Dec
McCown's Longspur												
Lapland Longspur												
Smith's Longspur												
Chestnut-collared Longspur												
Snow Bunting												
Bobolink												
Red-winged Blackbird												
Eastern Meadowlark												
Western Meadowlark												
Yellow-headed Blackbird												
Rusty Blackbird												
Brewer's Blackbird												
Great-tailed Grackle												
Common Grackle												
Brown-headed Cowbird												
Orchard Oriole												
Northern Oriole												
Purple Finch												
House Finch												
Red Crossbill												
White-winged Crossbill												
Common Redpoll												
Pine Siskin												
American Goldfinch												
Evening Grosbeak												
House Sparrow												
Eurasian Tree Sparrow												

Notes _____

_____

_____

_____

_____

hummingbirds at feeder

ne of the best places to look for birds is in one's yard (a term we use loosely to mean in the vicinity of one's home, perhaps even a nearby park). Because most people spend a lot of time at home, the probability is high that they will encounter numerous birds there. Many St. Louis birders have observed more than a hundred species of birds in (or from) their yard. Below are some keys to finding birds in your yard.

Look for them. They're on the ground, they're on the roof, they're in the trees. Look around. Look up; many species, especially hawks, geese, herons, and egrets, will only be seen from your yard as they pass overhead in spring and fall.

Listen for them. The songs and calls of birds are a good way to locate birds that might otherwise go unnoticed. With practice, most species can be identified by their songs and calls. Learn the vocalizations of the common birds and listen for unusual songs and calls. Some recordings of bird songs are described at the end of this chapter.

Be aware of the seasonal change. Every season brings different birds to our area (see **Seasonal Occurrence**). In late April and early May, insect-eating birds that wintered south of St. Louis arrive. Summer provides a time for birds to breed. The migration process works in reverse, but more slowly, in late August through November. Everybody knows that birds fly south for the winter, but for some species, St. Louis *is* south. Thus, cold weather brings many northern birds to the area that can only be seen in winter.

Study them. Keep your binoculars and field guide handy.

Attract them. Food, water (especially running water), plants, and nest boxes can attract birds. There are numerous detailed books and pamphlets available on this subject, but some considerations are presented below.

BIRDHOUSES

A few cavity-nesting birds can be enticed to nest in birdhouses. In our area, chickadees and wrens commonly nest in birdboxes. Some lucky box-builders have even attracted Eurasian Tree Sparrows. In rural areas, or suburban areas with open spaces like parks or golf courses, properly placed nest boxes can attract Eastern Bluebirds. Similarly, in open areas near water, Purple Martins may be attracted by communal nest boxes mounted on high poles away from trees, such as those at the Botanical Garden. Some suburbanites have been surprised to discover how easy it is to attract Eastern Screech-Owls with a large nest box. Be prepared to face the moral dilemma of what to do about the aggressive European Starlings and House Sparrows that will probably be the first to find your bird-house. Most species don't nest in cavities, but Eastern Phoebes, Barn Swallows, Blue Jays, and American Robins often build open nests on artificial platforms. Information on how to build and maintain birdhouses can be obtained from the Missouri and Illinois Departments of Conservation and in books available at garden stores.

FEEDERS

Many people enjoy feeding birds and watching the antics that inevitably occur at a bird feeder. Although bird seed can be bought at supermarkets, hardware stores, and nurseries, feeding birds is now so popular that there are special stores that offer a variety of products to help you attract birds to your yard. Some people feed birds all year long, but most wait for winter. Extreme cold weather or a snowfall or icestorm will often bring large numbers of seed-eating birds to your feeder since birds need extra energy in winter, and other food sources are concealed. Seed feeders come in a variety of shapes. Some are designed to attract only small birds like titmice and goldfinches while others are made for larger birds like cardinals and jays. Some people fight a life-long battle with squirrels; others capitulate by throwing cheap cracked corn on the ground to keep the squirrels from destroying the feeders, thereby also providing food for the ground feeding birds such as doves and juncos.

Hummingbirds can be attracted by sugar-water feeders that are sold at most nurseries and feed stores. Most sightings of hummingbirds at feeders occur in May, late August, and early September when Ruby-throated Hummingbirds migrate through the area. However, you may want to keep your feeder filled as late as November. Recently, some western humming-birds have visited Missouri feeders in October and November. There is no strong evidence that maintaining feeders into late fall entices hummingbirds to linger when they should be heading south.

Remember, your success at attracting birds depends not only on your feeder and the type of food you supply, but also on where you live and the habitat you provide. Different species will occur in the farmyards than in the city, and a different variety of birds can be expected in a wooded area with a nearby pond or stream than in a new subdivision with only a few trees and shrubs. Birds usually don't come to feeders unless there are nearby shrubs or trees in which to seek cover.

Insect-eating birds are not attracted to feeders, but will love the accouterments in your yard. Chimney Swifts may nest in your chimney, but they find their food on the wing.

Cedar Waxwings

Chimney Swifts

Mockingbirds and waxwings will be attracted to fruit-bearing trees and shrubs with berries. Migrating vireos and warblers will feed on insects in your trees, but they practically never come to seed feeders. Robins and other thrushes will find worms and grubs in your manicured lawn and will visit the bird bath, but they won't visit your seed feeder.

Below is a list of species that commonly visit feeders in the St. Louis area and types of food they prefer.

Species	Preferred food
Rock Dove	grain
Mourning Dove	millet
Ruby-throated Hummingbird	sugar water (May-September)
Downy Woodpecker	suet
Hairy Woodpecker	suet
Red-bellied Woodpecker	suet
Northern Flicker	suet
Blue Jay	sunflower seed
American Crow	suet, garbage
Black-capped Chickadee	sunflower seed
Carolina Chickadee	sunflower seed
Tufted Titmouse	sunflower seed
White-breasted Nuthatch	sunflower seed
Carolina Wren	sunflower seed, peanut butter
Northern Mockingbird	fruit, peanut butter, suet
European Starling	suet, peanut butter
Northern Cardinal	sunflower seed
Song Sparrow	millet
White-throated Sparrow	millet, sunflower seed
Dark-eyed Junco	sunflower seed
Common Grackle	sunflower seed, cracked corn
House Finch	thistle seed, sunflower seed
American Goldfinch	thistle seed, sunflower seed
House Sparrow	millet, bread, sunflower seed
Eurasian Tree Sparrow	thistle seed, sunflower seed

The species listed below may also be found at or near feeders, but they are uncommon, rare, or variable in abundance from year to year. Some are only likely to be seen in rural areas (R).

Species	Preferred food
Mallard	grain
Sharp-shinned Hawk	small birds at seed feeder
Cooper's Hawk	small birds at seed feeder
Ring-necked Pheasant (R)	corn, grain
Wild Turkey (R)	corn, grain
Red-headed Woodpecker (R)	suet
Pileated Woodpecker (R)	suet
Red-breasted Nuthatch	sunflower seed
Bewick's Wren (R)	sunflower seed
Rufous-sided Towhee	sunflower seed
Fox Sparrow (R)	sunflower seed, grain
Swamp Sparrow (R)	sunflower seed, grain
White-crowned Sparrow	sunflower seed, grain
Red-winged Blackbird	grain
Brown-headed Cowbird	grain
Northern Oriole	fruit (May-September)
Purple Finch	sunflower seed
Red Crossbill	sunflower seed
White-winged Crossbill	sunflower seed
Common Redpoll	thistle seed, sunflower seed
Pine Siskin	thistle seed, sunflower seed
Evening Grosbeak	sunflower seed

IDENTIFICATION AIDS

Below are some aids that are useful for identification of the birds of the St. Louis area.

Field Guides
Field Guide to the Birds of North America, 2nd Edition
- National Geographic Society
- 1987, National Geographic Society, Washington, 464 pages paper cover
- The National Geographic Guide has probably been the most popular all-round guide for the active birder since its 1984 debut.

A Field Guide to the Birds East of the Rockies, 4th edition
(recent editions simply say *"Eastern Birds"* on the cover)
- Roger Tory Peterson
- 1980, Houghton Mifflin Co., Boston, 384 pages
- Flexible "field" cover or hardcover
- The "Peterson System" of pinpointing key field marks is an invaluable aid to beginners. Because this book only covers birds of eastern and central U. S., it is somewhat less confusing than the National Geographic and Golden guides.

(A Guide to Field Identification) Birds of North America, Expanded and Revised Edition
- Chandler S. Robbins, Bertel Bruun, and Herbert S. Zim
- 1983, Golden Press, New York, 360 pages paper or hardcover
- The "Golden Guide" is a basic but valuable field guide.

Sound Recordings of Bird Songs and Calls
Guide to Bird Sounds
- Cornell Laboratory of Ornithology, 1985
- Two cassette tapes in case
- Keyed to paged numbers of the National Geographic *Field Guide to the Birds of North America*. Calls, songs, trills, and other sounds are recorded for 179 species.

Eastern/Central Bird Songs (also known as *A Field Guide to Bird Songs*)
- Roger Tory Peterson, ed., 1983/1990, Peterson Field Guides, Houghton Mifflin
- Two cassette tapes or one compact disc
- Keyed by page numbers to the 4th edition of Peterson's *A Field Guide to the Birds*; songs and calls are recorded for over 250 species.

Birding by Ear; Guide to Bird Song Identification
- Richard K. Walton and Robert W. Larson, 1989
- Three cassette tapes and 64-page booklet
- A comparative guide to 85 species occurring in the eastern and central United States.

Know Your Bird Sounds, Vol. 1 & Vol. 2
- Lang Elliot, 1991
- Each volume consists of one 65-minute cassette tape
- Volume 1 contains sounds of 35 species of residential settings, city parks, and urban areas while Volume 2 has sounds of 35 species of the countryside.

All of the above identification aids can be purchased from ABA Sales (operated by the American Birding Association), P. O. Box 6599, Colorado Springs, CO, 80934. The toll-free number is (800) 634-7736. The books are available locally in well-stocked bookstores and some of the recordings can be obtained at the book shop at the Missouri Botanical Garden.

sculptures and bald cypress, Missouri Botanical Garden

References and Bibliography

- A. O. U. (1983) *Checklist of North American Birds,* Sixth Edition, American Ornithologists Union.

- A. O. U. (1993) *39th Supplement to the Checklist of North American Birds, Auk* 110, 675-682.

- Anderson D. (1994) Missing Petrel Specimen Found. Identification Confirmed. *The Bluebird* 61, 13-14.

- Anderson R. A. and Bauer P. E. (1968) *A Guide to Finding Birds in the St. Louis Area,* Webster Groves Nature Study Society, Saint Louis.

- Bohlen H. D. and Zimmerman W. (1989) *The Birds of Illinois,* Indiana University Press, Bloomington and Indianapolis.

- Hayman P., Marchant J., and Prater T. (1986) *Shorebirds: An Identification Guide to the Waders of the World,* Houghton Mifflin, New York.

- Jones S. P. (1943) *Migratory and Permanent Resident Birds in the St. Louis Region,* St. Louis Bird Club.

- Kaufman K. (1990) *A Field Guide to Advanced Birding,* Houghton Mifflin, New York.

- Ridgway R. (1895) *The Ornithology of Illinois,* Part 1, Vol. 2, State Laboratory of Natural History, Springfield.

- Robbins M. B. and Easterla D. A. (1992) *Birds of Missouri,* University of Missouri Press, Columbia and London.

- Widmann O. (1907) *A Preliminary Catalog of the Birds of Missouri,* Academy of Science, St. Louis.

- Widmann O. (1909) Summer Birds of Shaw's Garden, *Twentieth Annual Report of the Missouri Botanical Garden,* 59-62.

- Wilhelm E. J. Jr. (1958) *Birds of the St. Louis Area,* St. Louis Audubon Society.

Index

Hints:

Look up general, then specific, i.e., "Warbler, Prairie," "Arboretum, Shaw," or "River, Missouri."
Bold-faced numbers indicate pages of primary discussion.
Bold italics indicate page number of **SEASONAL OCCURRENCE** bar graph for birds, or map(s) for birding locations.
Species names start with Capital Letters.

- A -

A. O. U.: see American Ornithologists Union
accipiter, accipiters: 25, 64, **100**
Airport
  Lambert: *18*, *19*, 26, 145, 150
  Scott Air Force Base: 152
  Smartt Field: see Airport, St. Charles Co.
  St. Charles: *18*, *34*, **39**, 82, 83, 105, 107, 128, 140, 141, 152
  St. Charles Co.: *34*, **40**, 140, 152
airports: 110, 140
Alabama: 89
Alta Villa: *34*, **41**, 147
Alton: 3, *19*, 36, 59, 86, 87, 88, 102, 104, 111, 113, 114, 125, 147
American Ornithologists Union: 85, 88, 147
Anhinga: 80, **89**, *161*
Arboretum, Shaw: **17**, 20, **52-54**, 82, 83, 99, 101, 103, 117, 119, 124, 126, 131, 132, 133, 134, 135, 136, 138, 143, 153
Arch, Gateway: 4, **31**, 147
Archery Range: 48
Audubon Society: V, 9, 12, 13, 23
Avocet, American: 38, 64, **106**, *164*

- B -

Barge Terminal, Alton: *34*, **35**, 66
Barracks, Jefferson: *19*, 32, 91, 150
Batchtown: 82
Bay, Ellis: *35*, 36
Big Day: 12
Bim's Place: **63**, 147
Bittern
  American: **90**, *161*
  Least: 44, 51, 70, **90**, *161*
bittern, bitterns: 44, 83
Blackbird
  Brewer's: 40, 42, 51, **142**, *173*
  Red-winged: **141**, *173*, 179
  Rusty: **141**, *173*
  Yellow-headed: 4, 44, 70, **141**, *173*
blackbird, blackbirds: 41, 42, 44
  see also:
    Cowbird, Brown-headed: **142**
    Grackle, Common: **142**
    Starling, European: **128**
Bluebird, Eastern: 29, 53, 56, 77, **126**, *169*, 176
Bobolink: 27, 44, **141**, *173*
Bobwhite, Northern: 54, 55, 64, 70, **103**, *164*
bookstore: 31, 181
Botanical Garden
  arboretum: see Arboretum, Shaw
  Missouri: 31, 53, 122, 151, 181
Brant: 77, 80, **94**, *162*
Breeding Bird Atlas Project: 11
Breeding Bird Survey: 11

bridge
  Blanchette Memorial: 148
  Chain of Rocks: 67
  Clark: *65*, 66, 148
  Daniel Boone: 149
  Eades: 31
  Jefferson Barracks: 77, *78*, 81
  McKinley: 65
  Poplar St.: 152
brushpile: 24, 148
Brussels: *58*, 63
Bufflehead: **98**, *163*
Bullfinch: 5
Bunting
  Indigo: 44, 56, **136**, *171*
  Lark: **138**, *172*
  Lazuli: **136**, *171*
  Snow: 50, 75, **141**, 156, *173*
Busch: see Conservation Area

- C -

CA: see Conservation Area
camping, campgrounds: 30, 55, 56, 59, 60, 70, 75, 81
Canal
  Cahokia: *68*, 70
  Chain of Rocks: 67
Canvasback: 52, 75, **96**, 157, *162*
Cardinal, Northern: 1, 25, **135**, *171*, 178
Carlyle: *72*, 73
Catbird, Gray: **127**, *169*
causeway: *68*, 69
cemeteries: 137, 143
  Bellefontaine: *19*, **31**, *34*, 143, 147
  Calvary: *19*, 31, *34*
  Jefferson National: **32**, 150
Chaffinch: 5
Chain of Rocks: 3, 31, *34*, **66**, 82, 91, 98, 108, 110, 113, 120, 148
Chat, Yellow-breasted: 29, 50, 53, **135**, *171*
Chautauqua: *34*, 65
Chickadee
  Black-capped: 4, 64, **123**, *168*, 178
  Carolina: 4, 25, **123**, *168*, 178
chicken, chickens, see
  Greater Prairie-Chicken: 103
Christmas Bird Count: 9, 10, 11, 91, 121, 125, 148, 156
  Orchard Farm: 42
  Pere Marquette: 60
  Weldon Spring: 50
Chuck-will's-widow: 29, 117, *167*
Chukar: 103
Clifton Terrace: 65
Collinsville: 10
Columbia: 77, 78

Authors

Connie Alwood is a past president of the Webster Groves Nature Study Society (WGNSS). When not birding, he teaches English at McCluer High School.

Dick Anderson, who is retired from the industrial electric supply business, has attempted serious birding in St. Louis since 1950. He joined the WGNSS in 1951, serving later as president. He has been active in compiling state and St. Louis bird checklists since 1958, has edited the Seasonal Survey for *The Bluebird* and *American Birds*, off and on, since 1961, and is currently a member of the Missouri Bird Record Committee.

Paul Bauer has been birding in St. Louis since 1947. In his remaining spare time, he has served as president and in other offices for the WGNSS, the Audubon Society of Missouri, the St. Louis Audubon Society, and also as regional director for the American Birding Association. Paul is a licensed professional engineer, now retired, so business no longer gets in the way of birding and nature photography.

Randy Korotev, who is a planetary geochemist at Washington University, has studied the spring migration through Forest Park and surveyed breeding birds in rural Illinois since 1979. He also compiles a Christmas Bird Count.

Jack Van Benthuysen has been a beginning birder since 1941. In 1990 he retired from an electrical engineering business and has been able to devote almost full time to furthering his birding knowledge.

Artists

Jim Ziebol is one of St. Louis' most active birders and butterfly observers. **Carmen Patterson**, who was the St. Louis area coordinator for the Missouri Breeding Bird Atlas Project, now lives and birds in California. **Chuck Witcher** is an active wildlife artist and retired commercial artist.

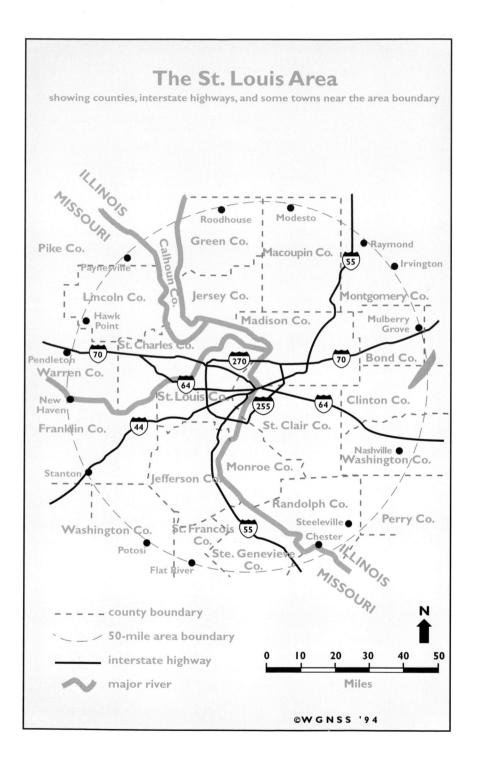

The St. Louis Area

showing counties, interstate highways, and some towns near the area boundary

ILLINOIS
MISSOURI

Roodhouse
Modesto

Green Co.

Macoupin Co.
Raymond
Irvington

Pike Co.
Paynesville
Calhoun Co.

Lincoln Co.
Jersey Co.
Montgomery Co.

Hawk Point
Madison Co.
Mulberry Grove

St. Charles Co.
70
Pendleton
270
70
Bond Co.

Warren Co.
64
New Haven
St. Louis Co.
255
64
Clinton Co.

Franklin Co.
44
St. Clair Co.

Stanton
Monroe Co.
Nashville
Washington Co.

Jefferson Co.

Washington Co.
Randolph Co.
Perry Co.

St. Francois Co.
55
Steeleville
Chester
ILLINOIS
MISSOURI

Potosi
Ste. Genevieve Co.

Flat River

- - - - - county boundary

〜〜〜 50-mile area boundary

──── interstate highway

〜〜〜 major river

N

| 0 | 10 | 20 | 30 | 40 | 50 |

Miles

©WGNSS '94